Mindful Designs

A Unique, Relaxing Adult Coloring Book for Stress Relief and Anxiety

Illustrated By:
Amelia Wells

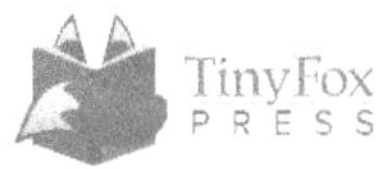

A Tiny Fox Press Book

ISBN: 978-1-946501-64-6

Find More Coloring Books By Amelia At:
www.tinyfoxpress.com

Tiny Fox Press LLC
North Port, FL

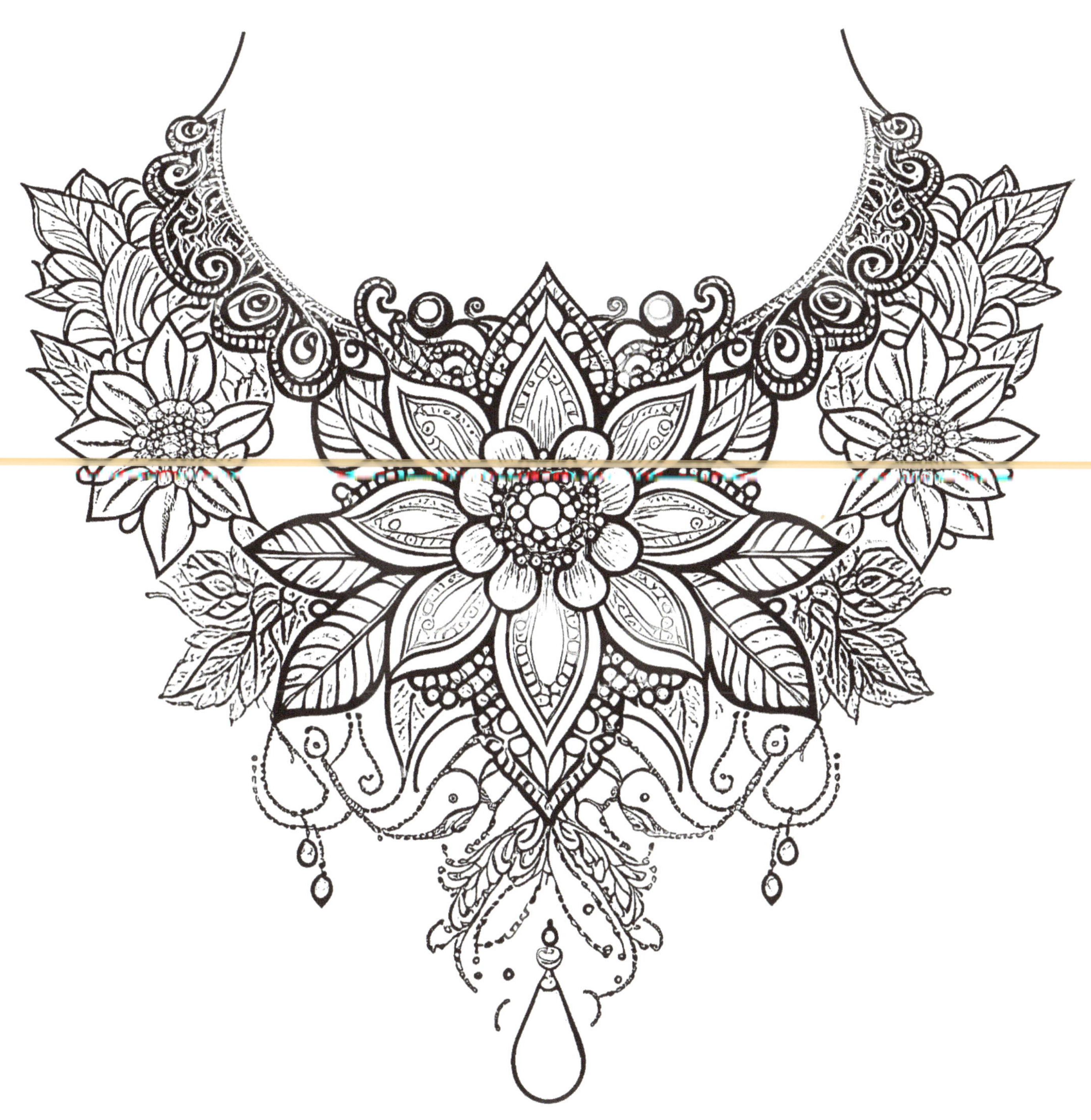

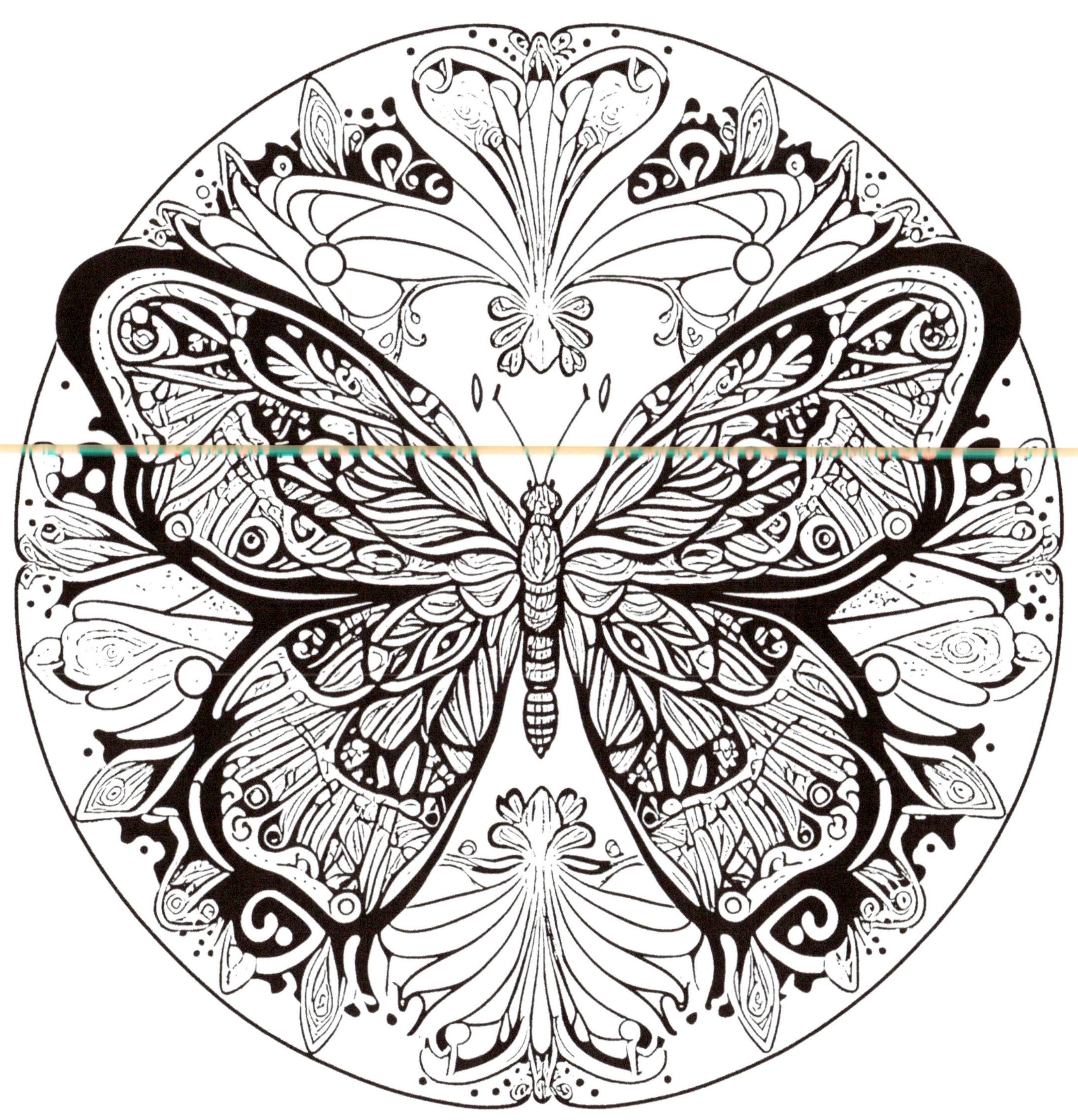

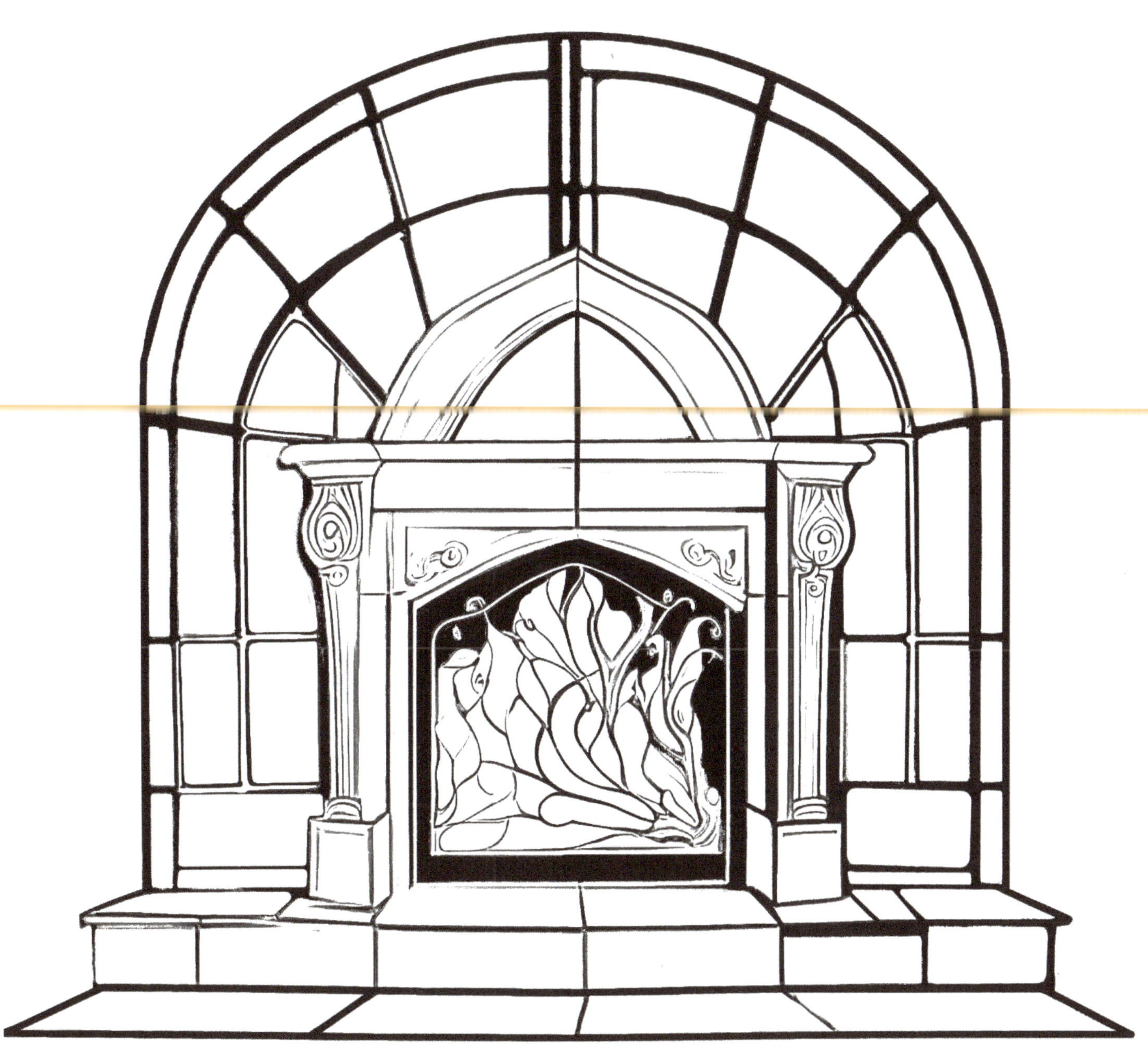

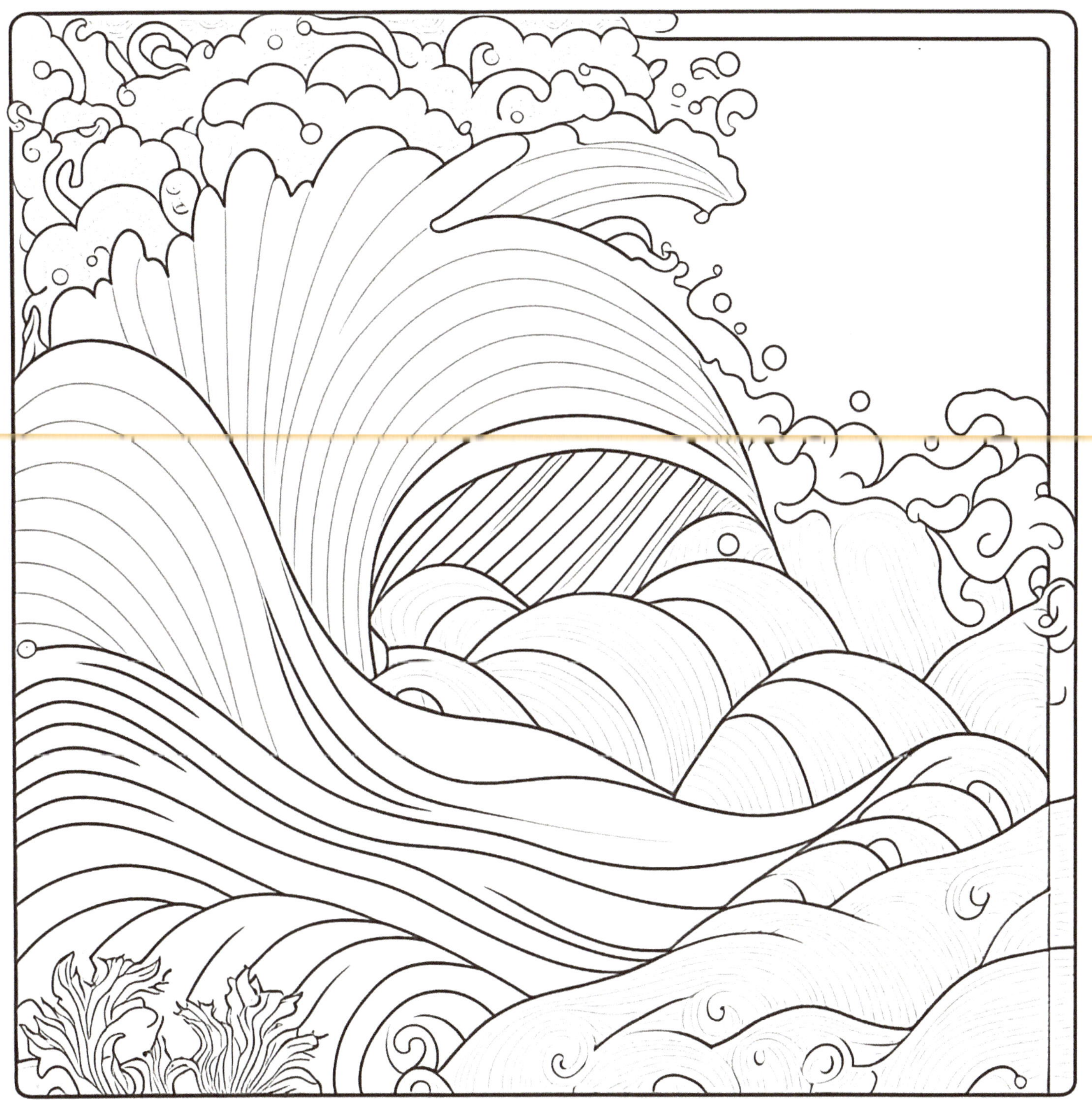

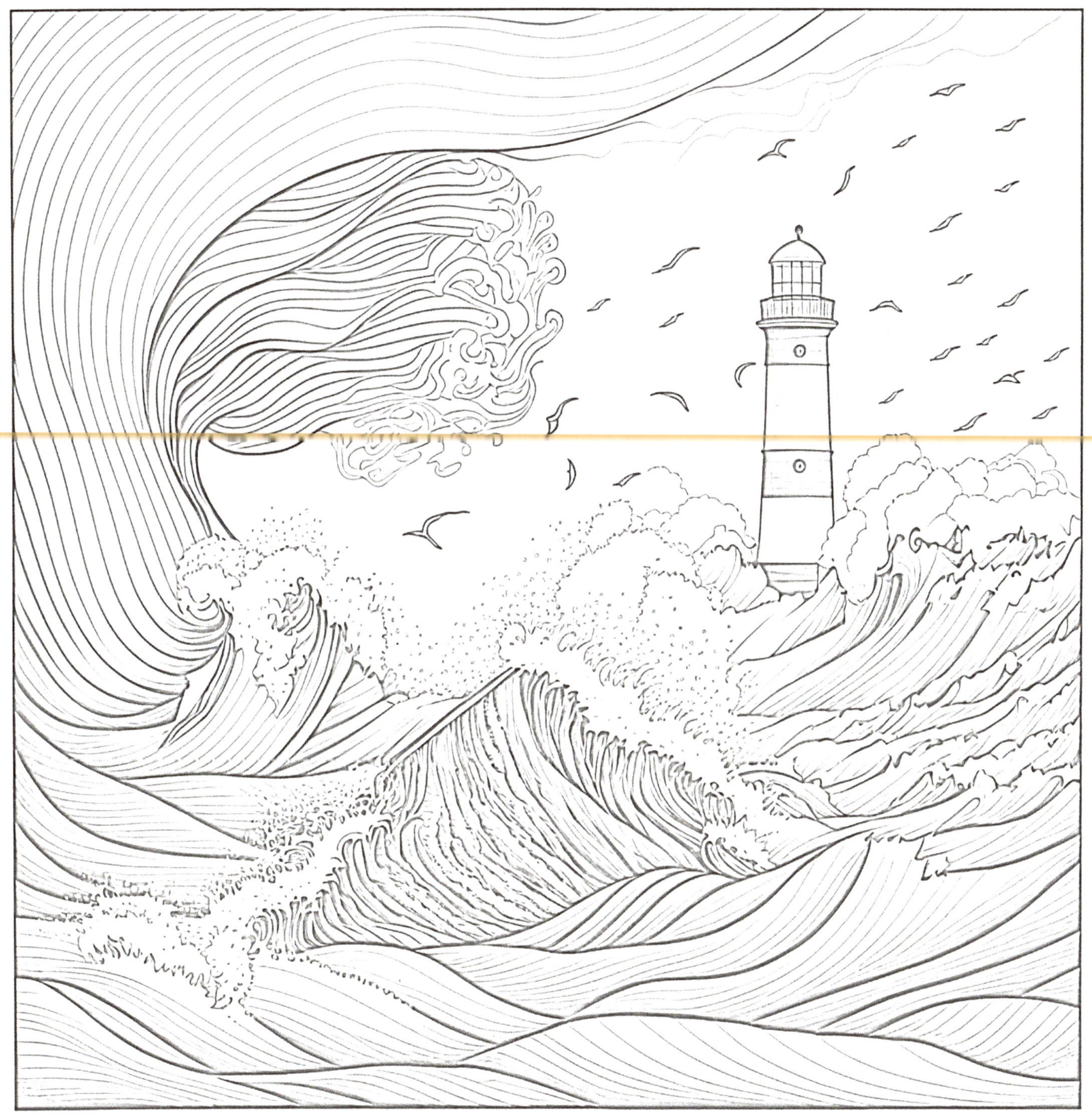

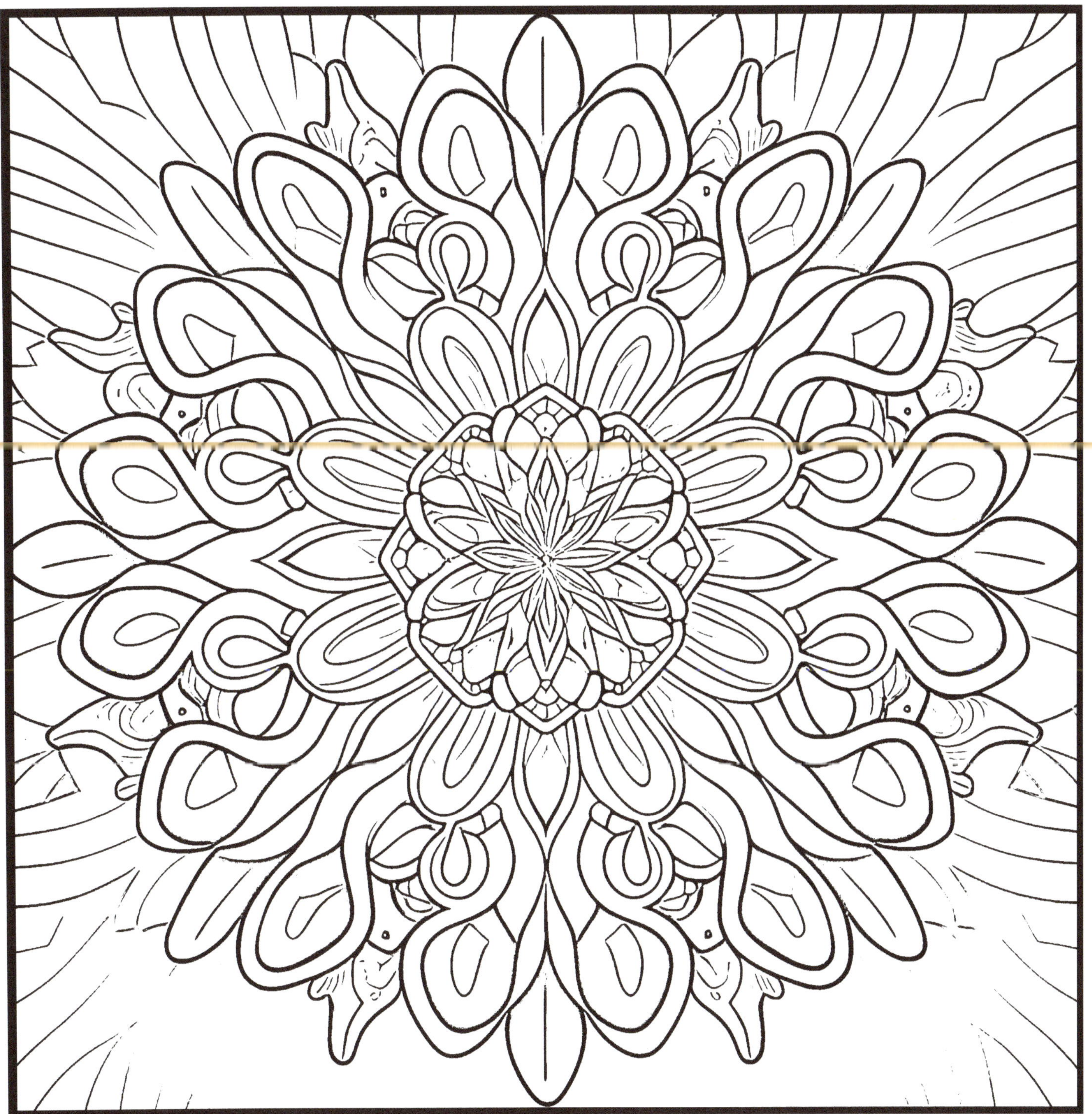

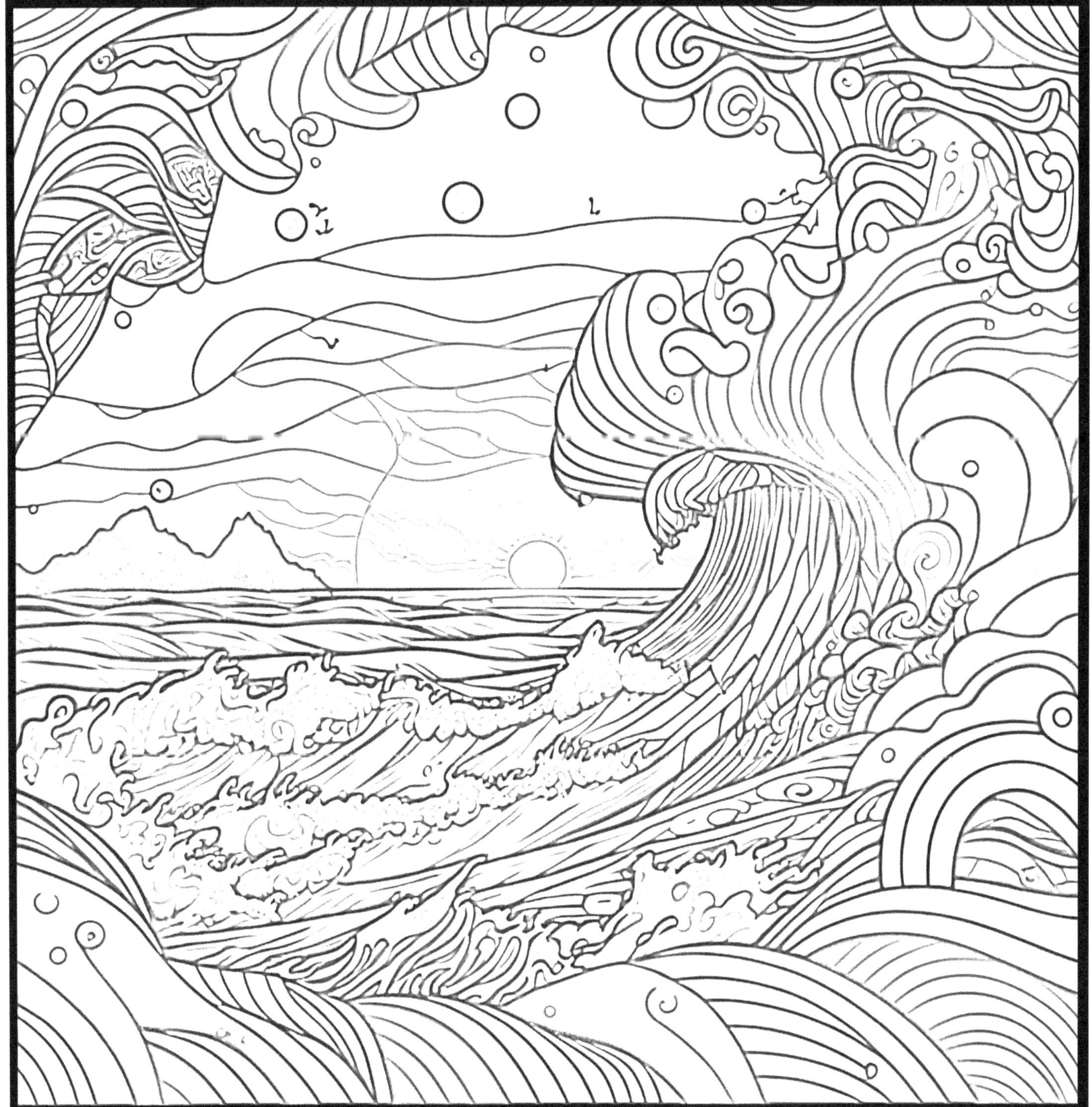

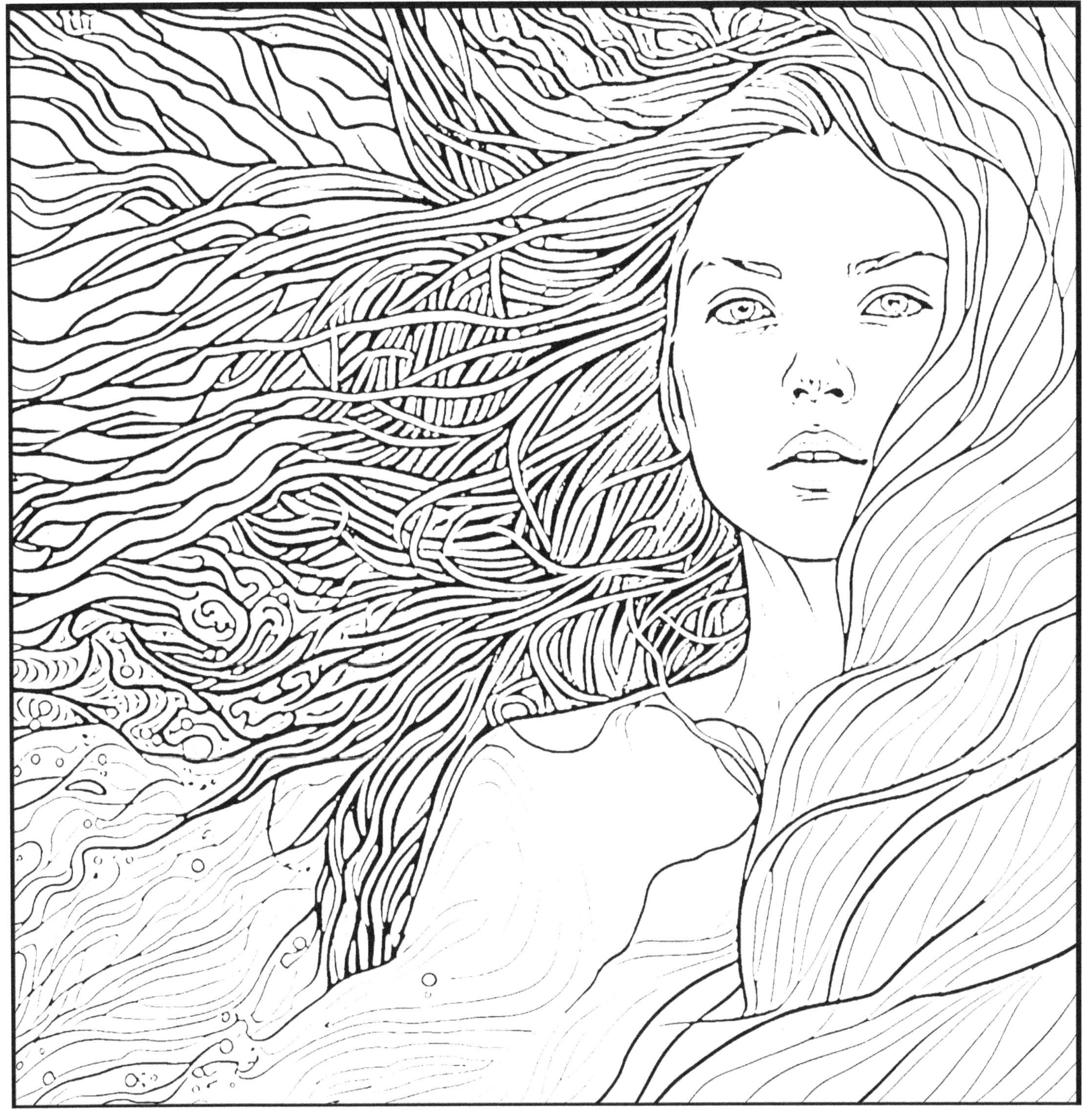

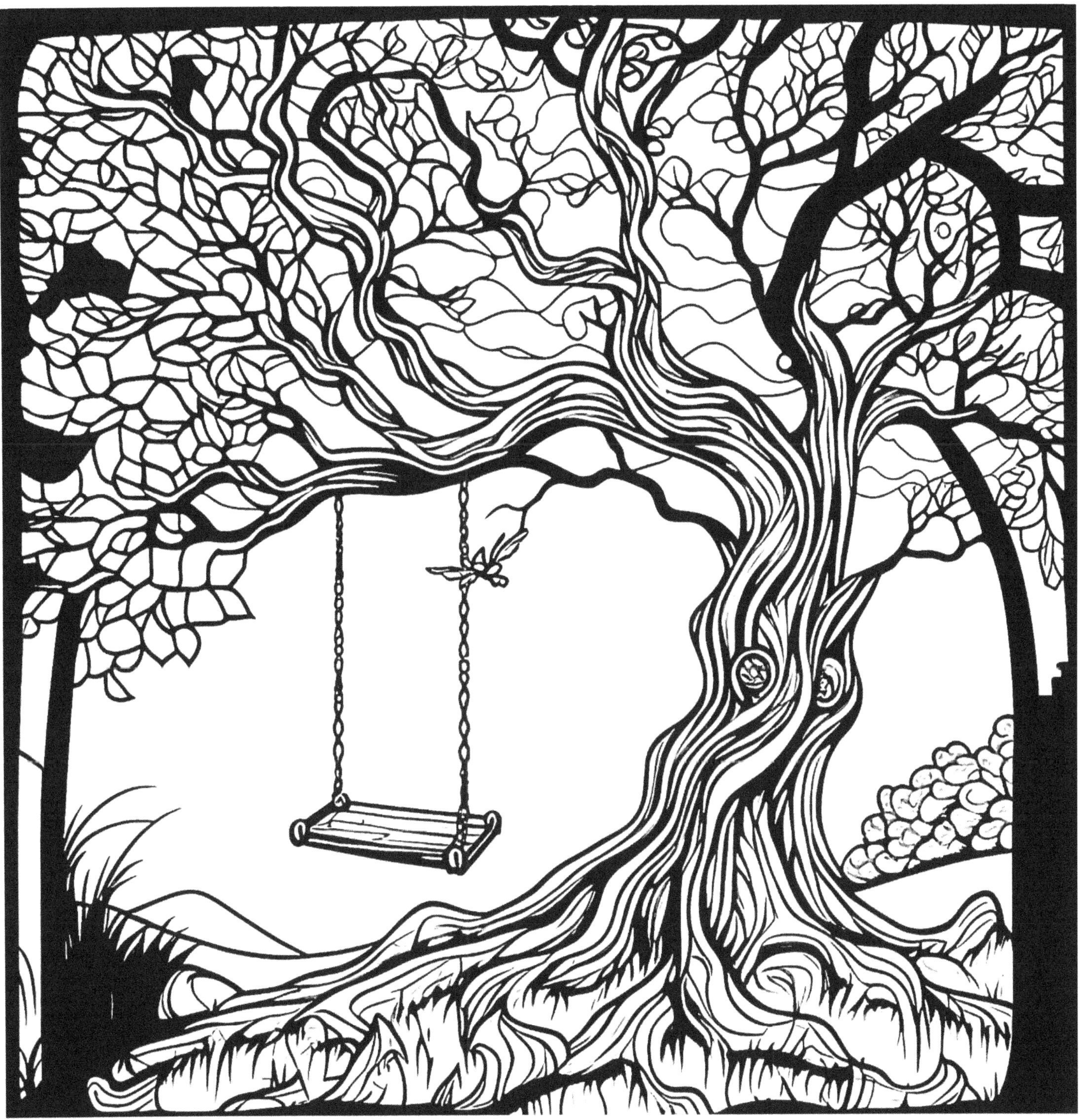

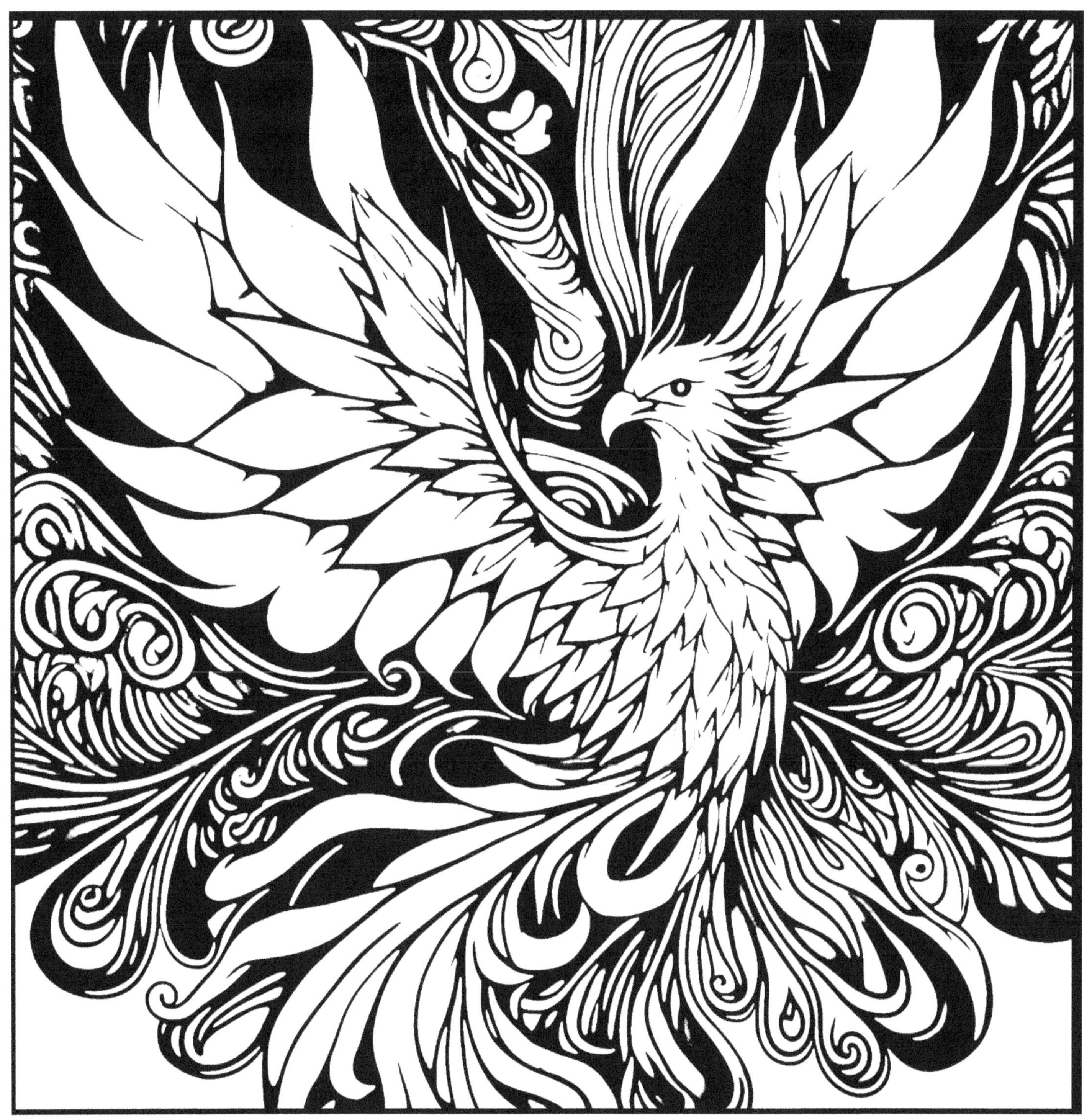

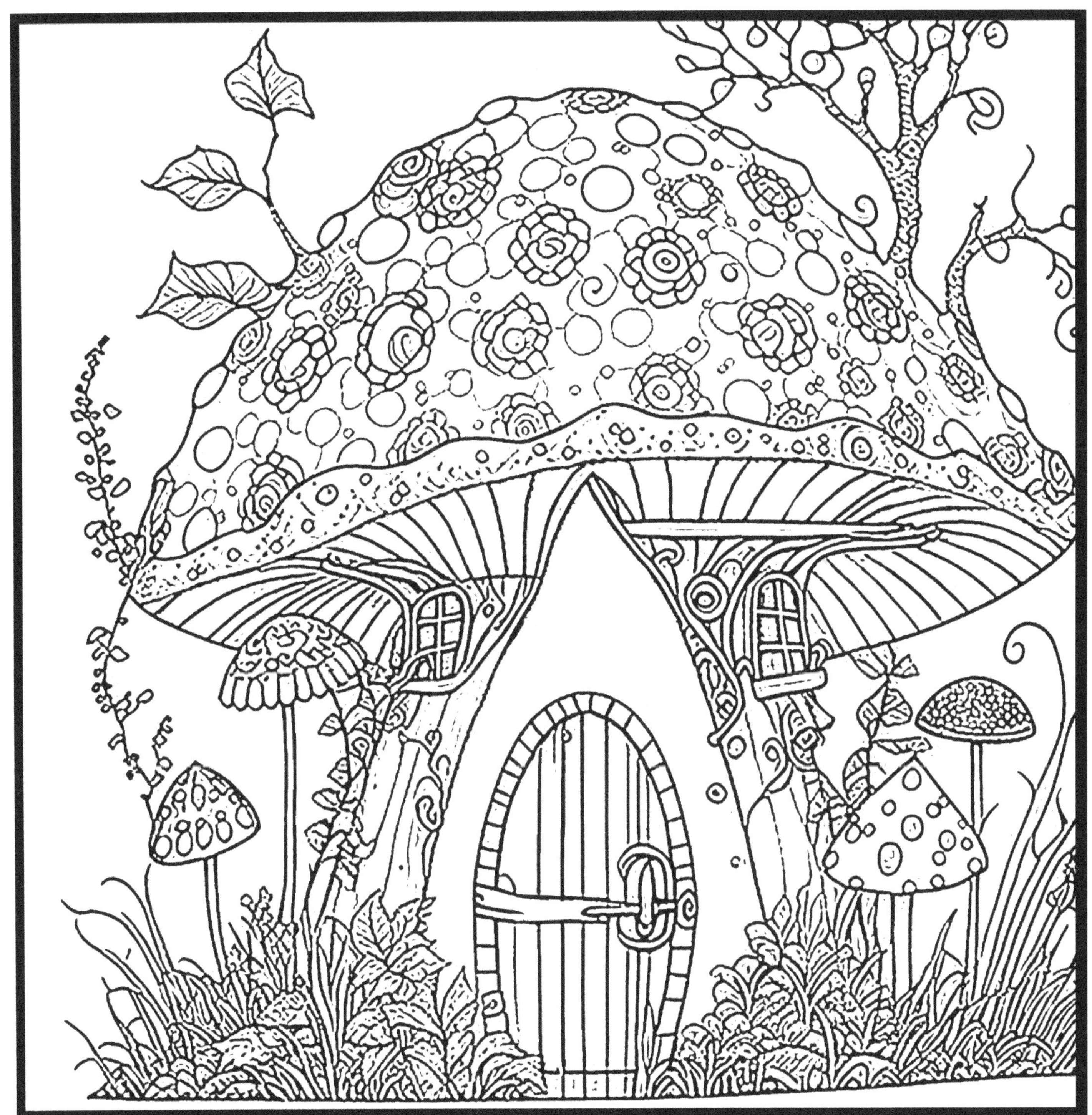

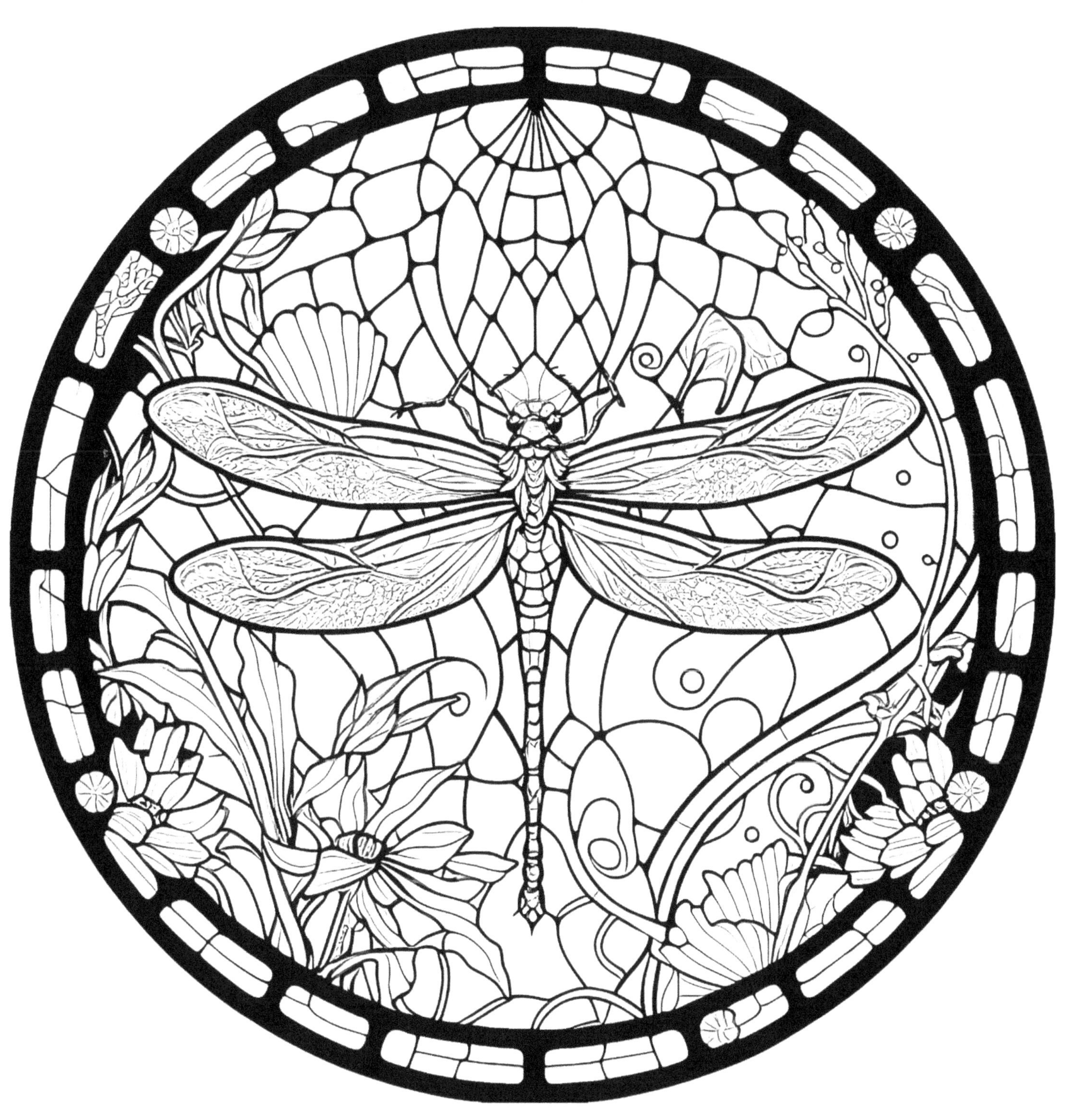

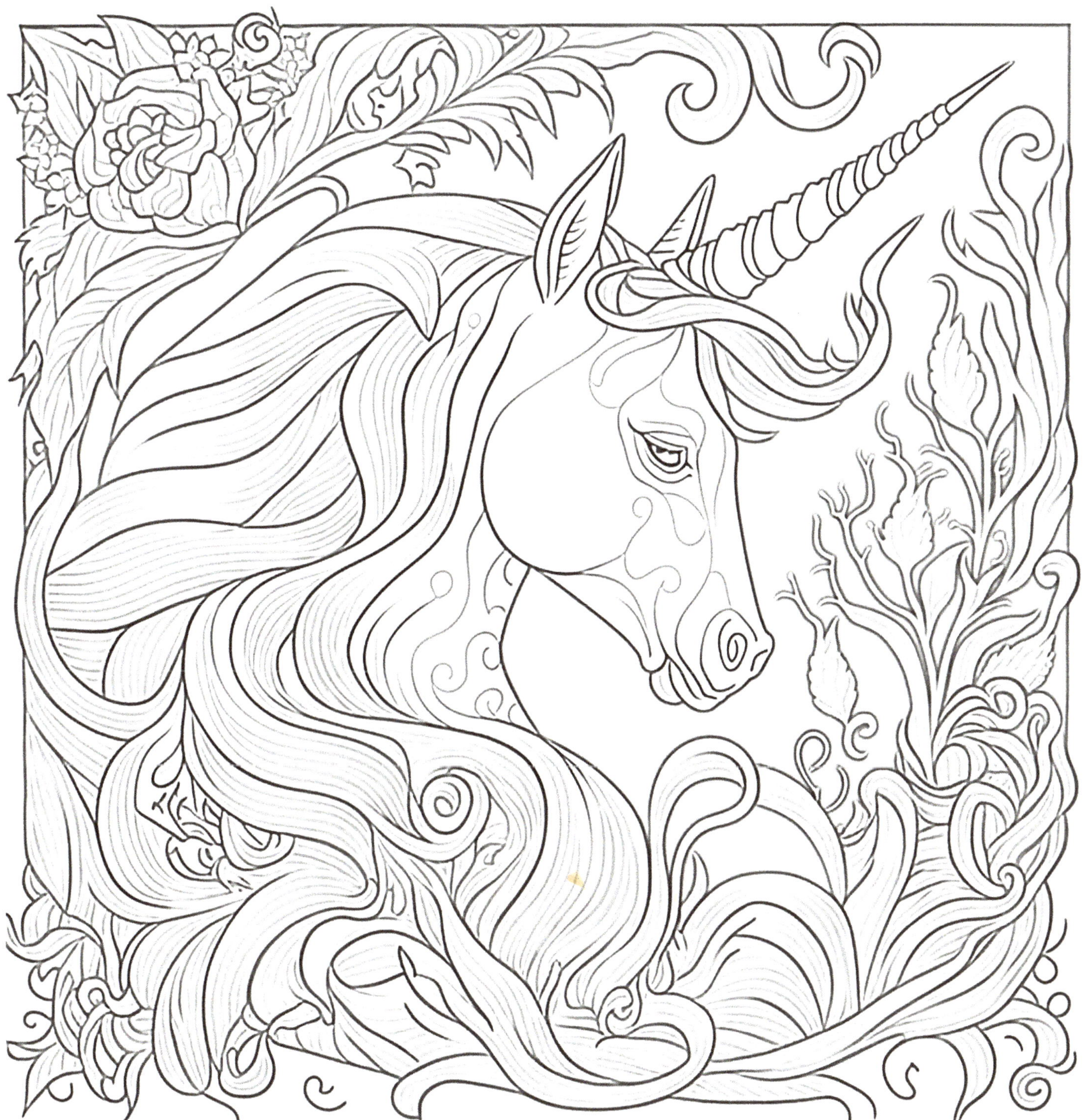

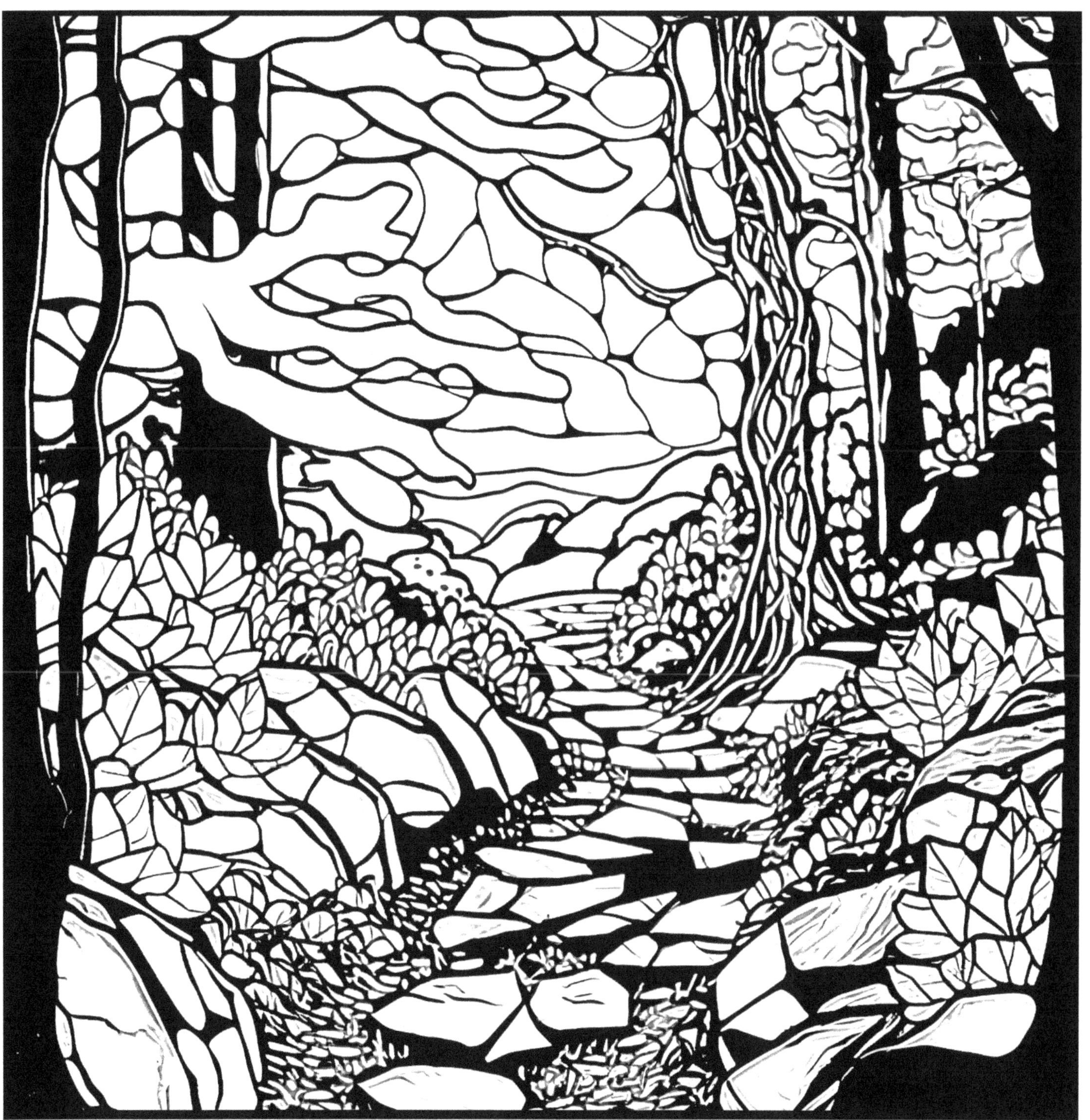

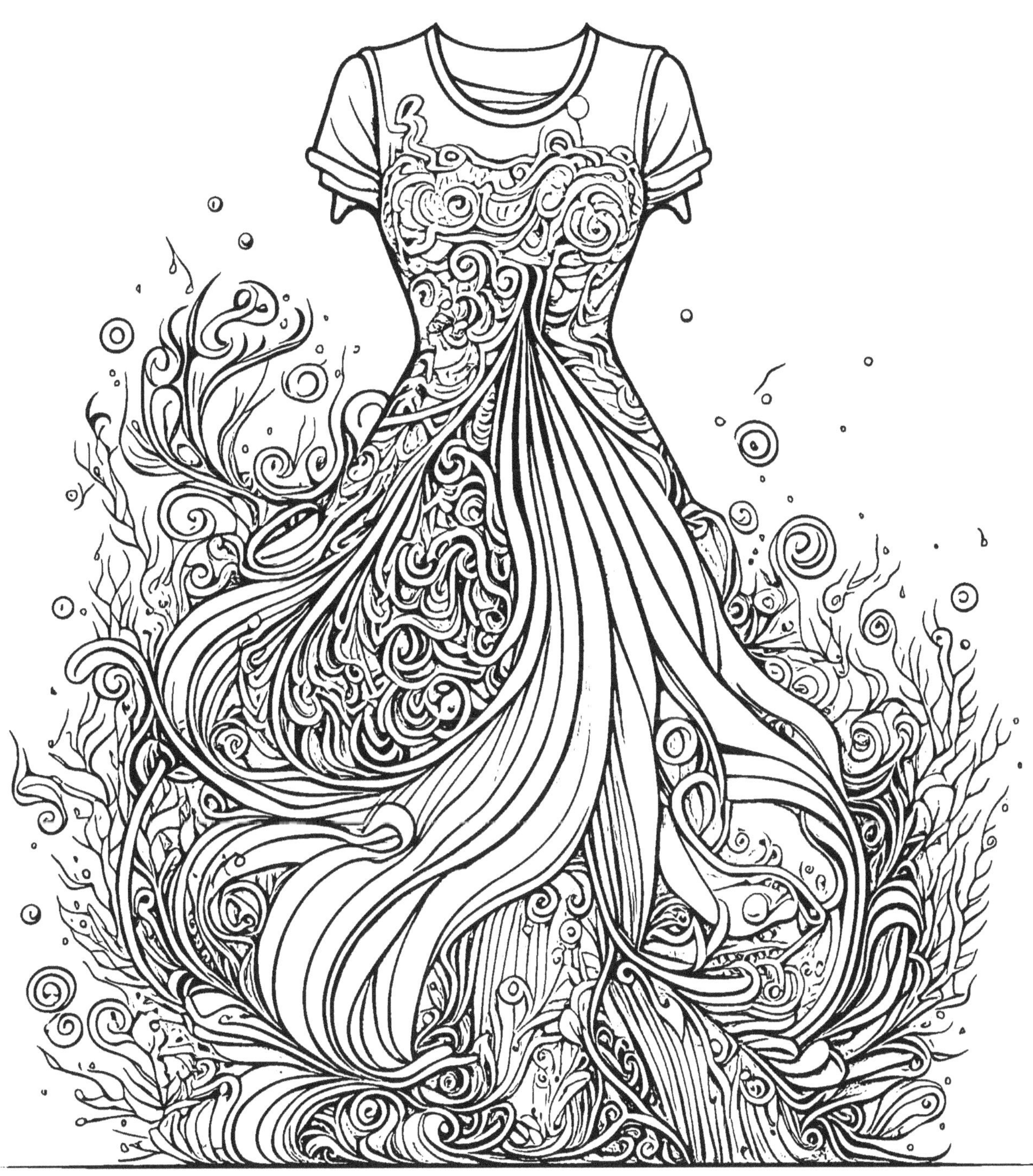

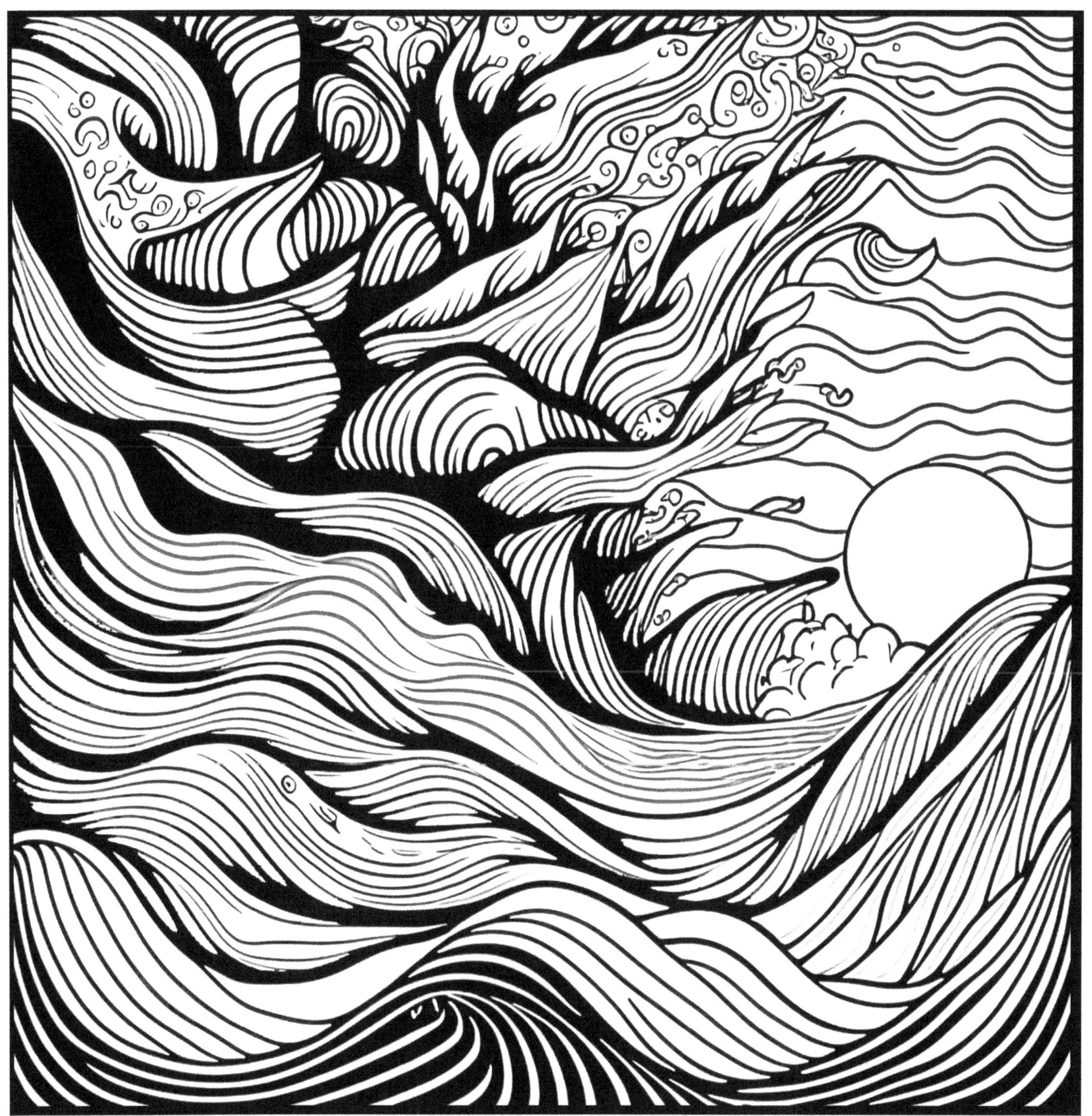

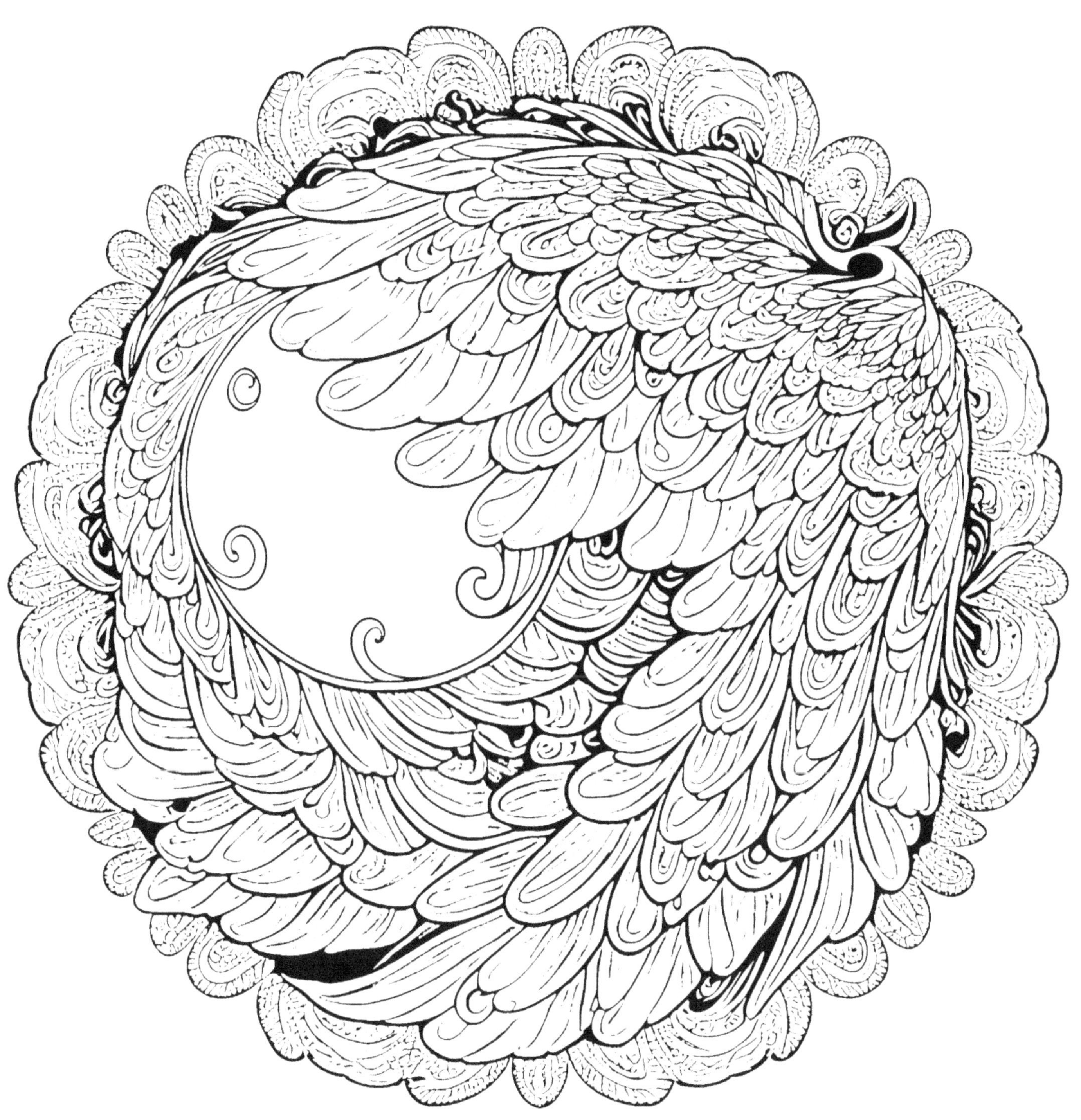

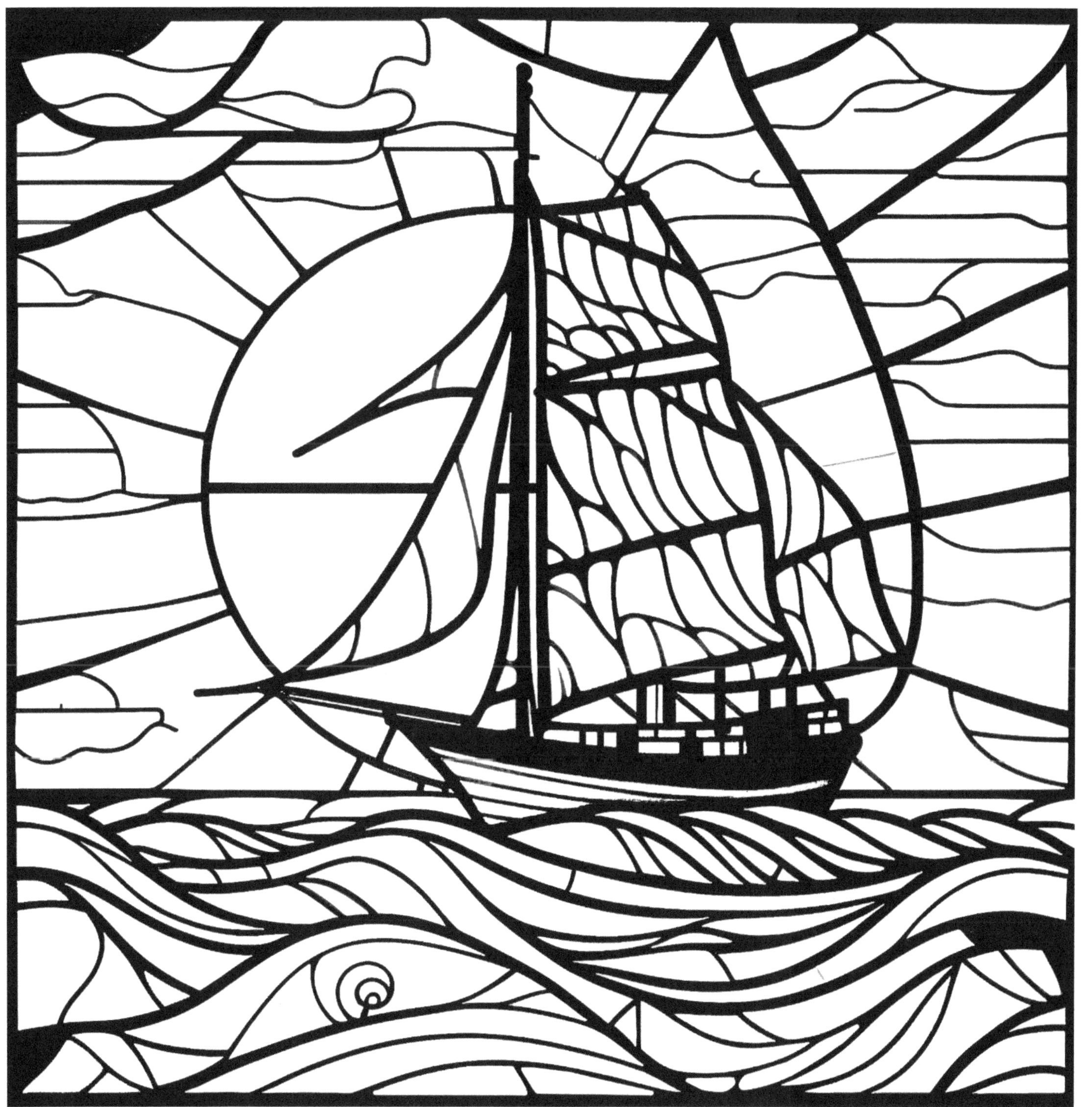

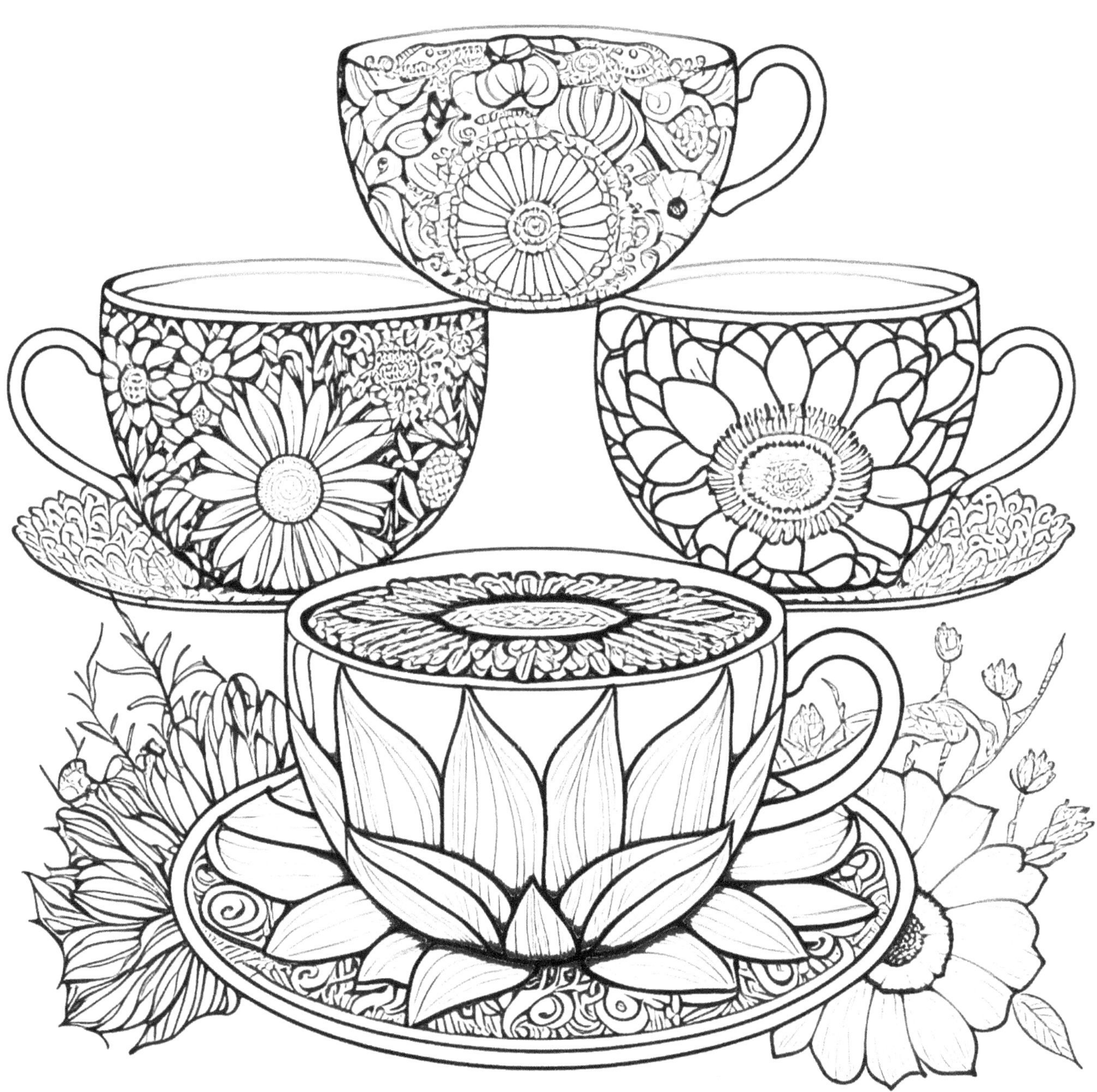

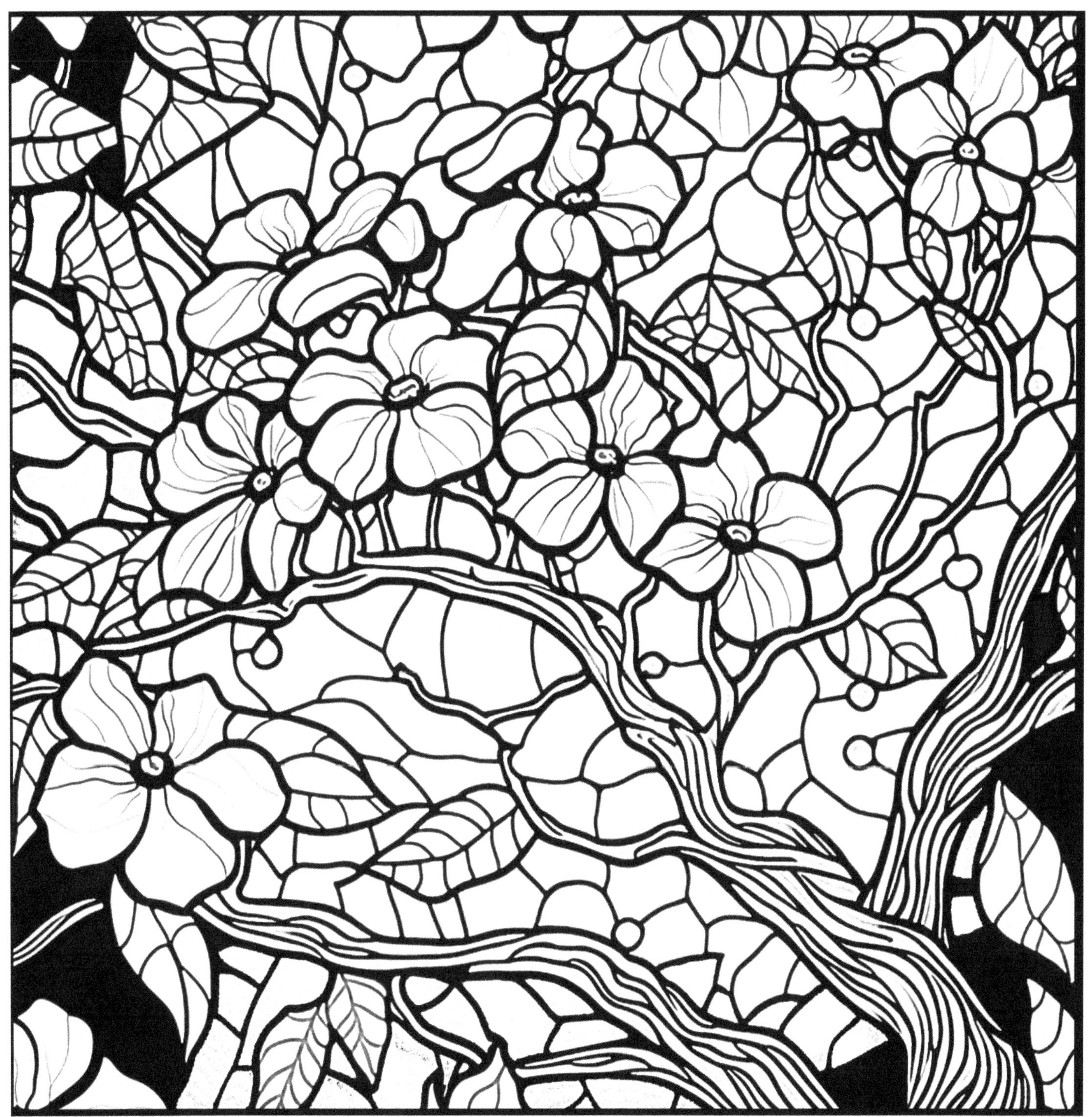

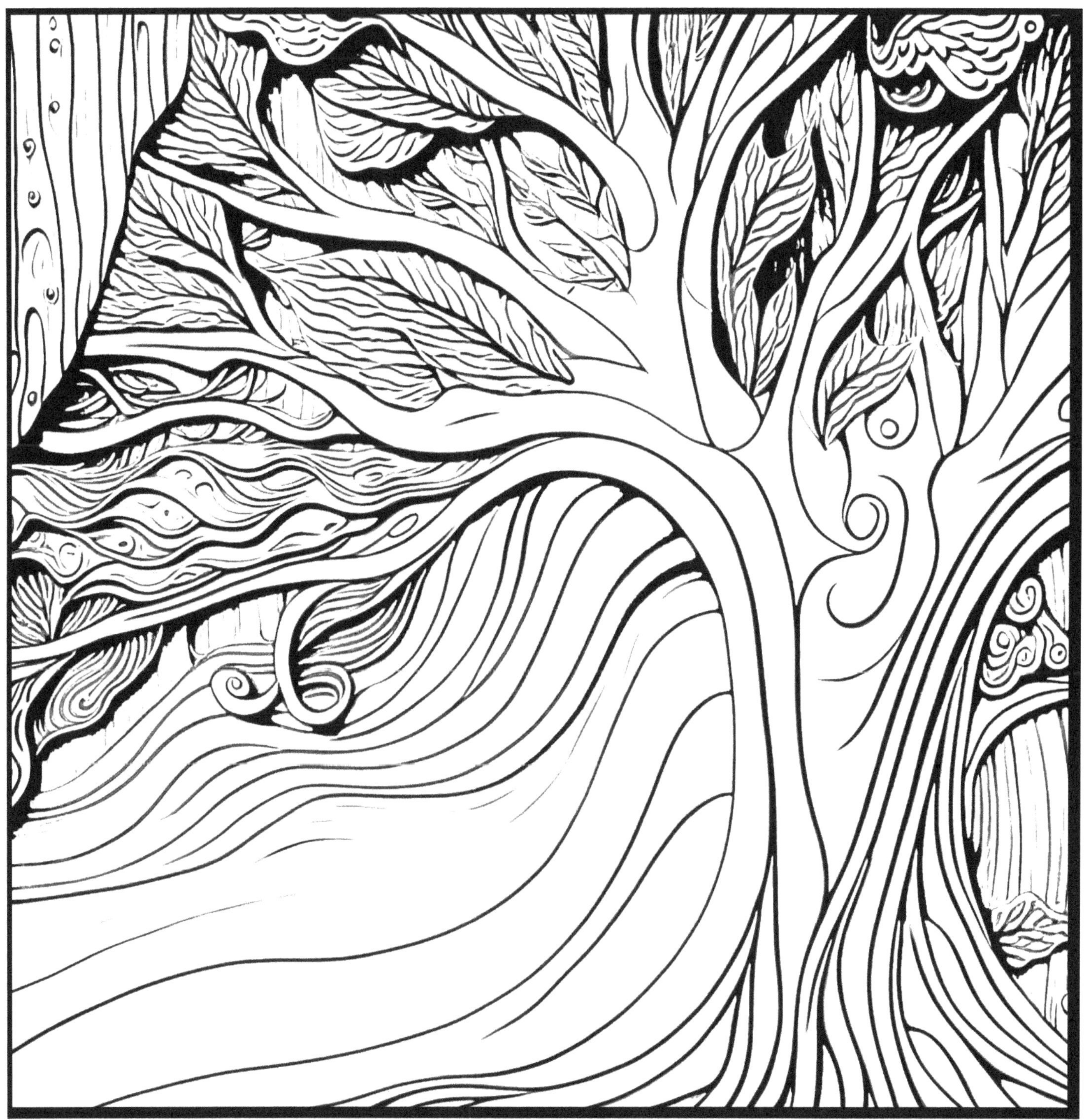

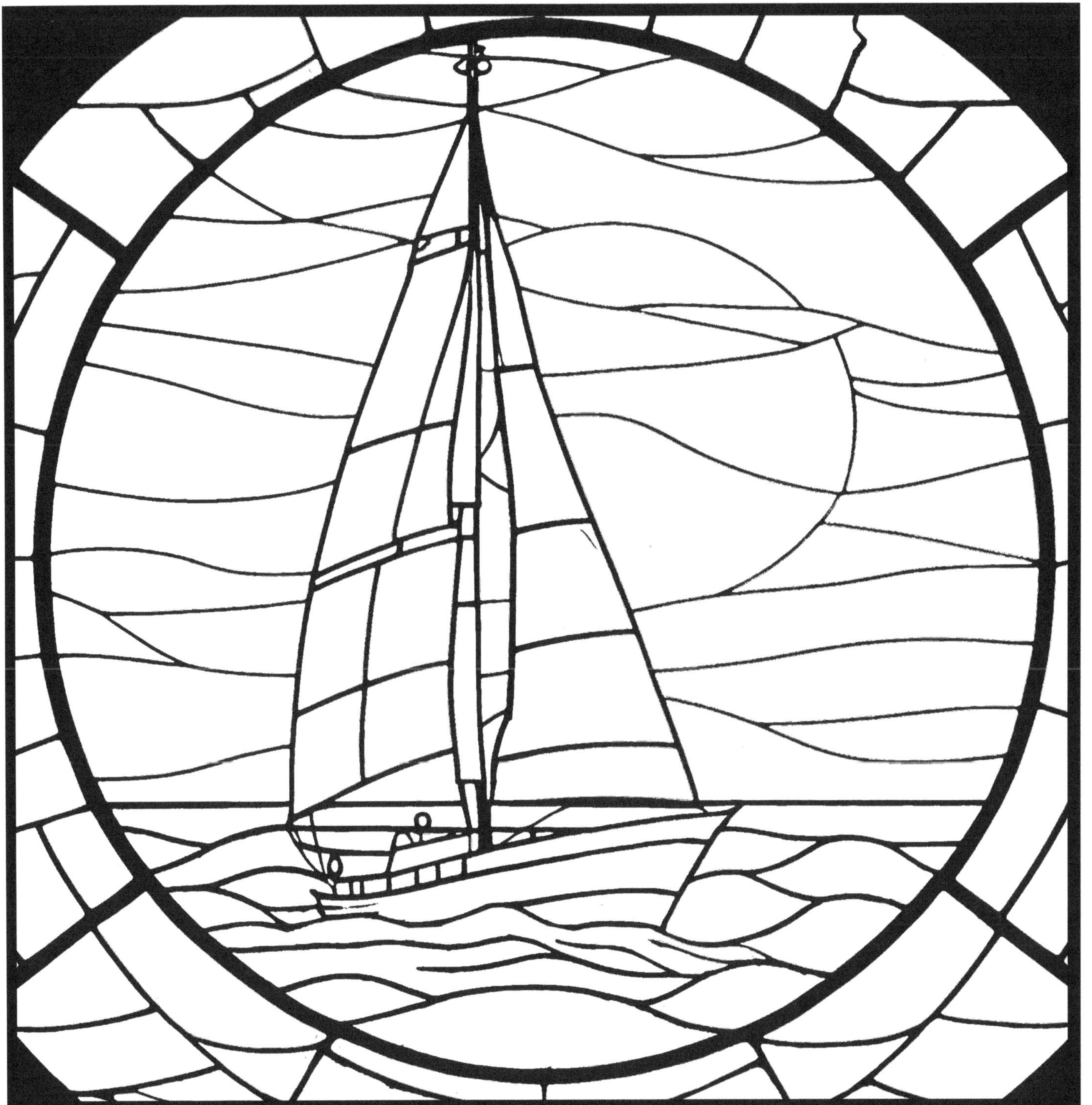

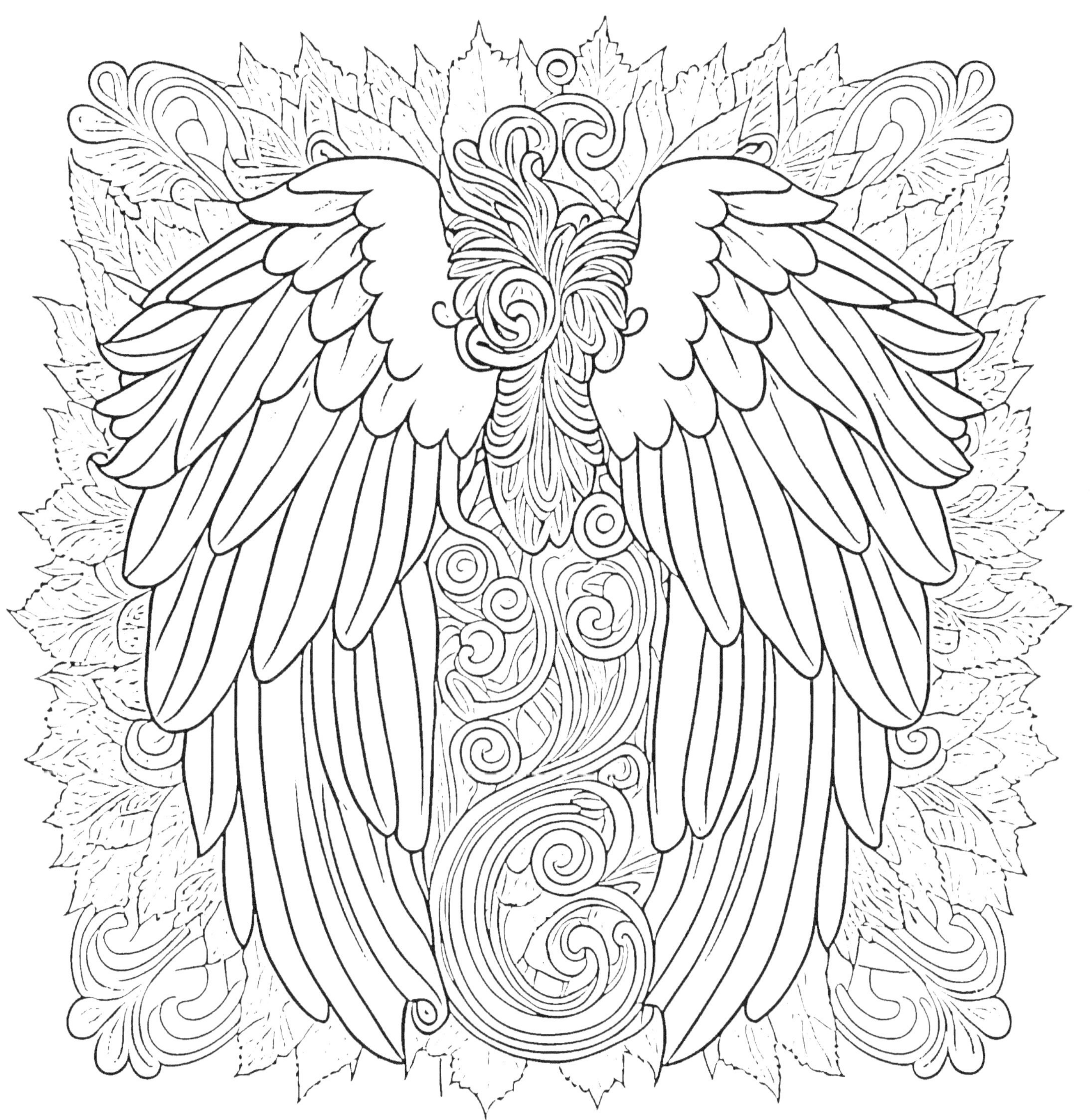

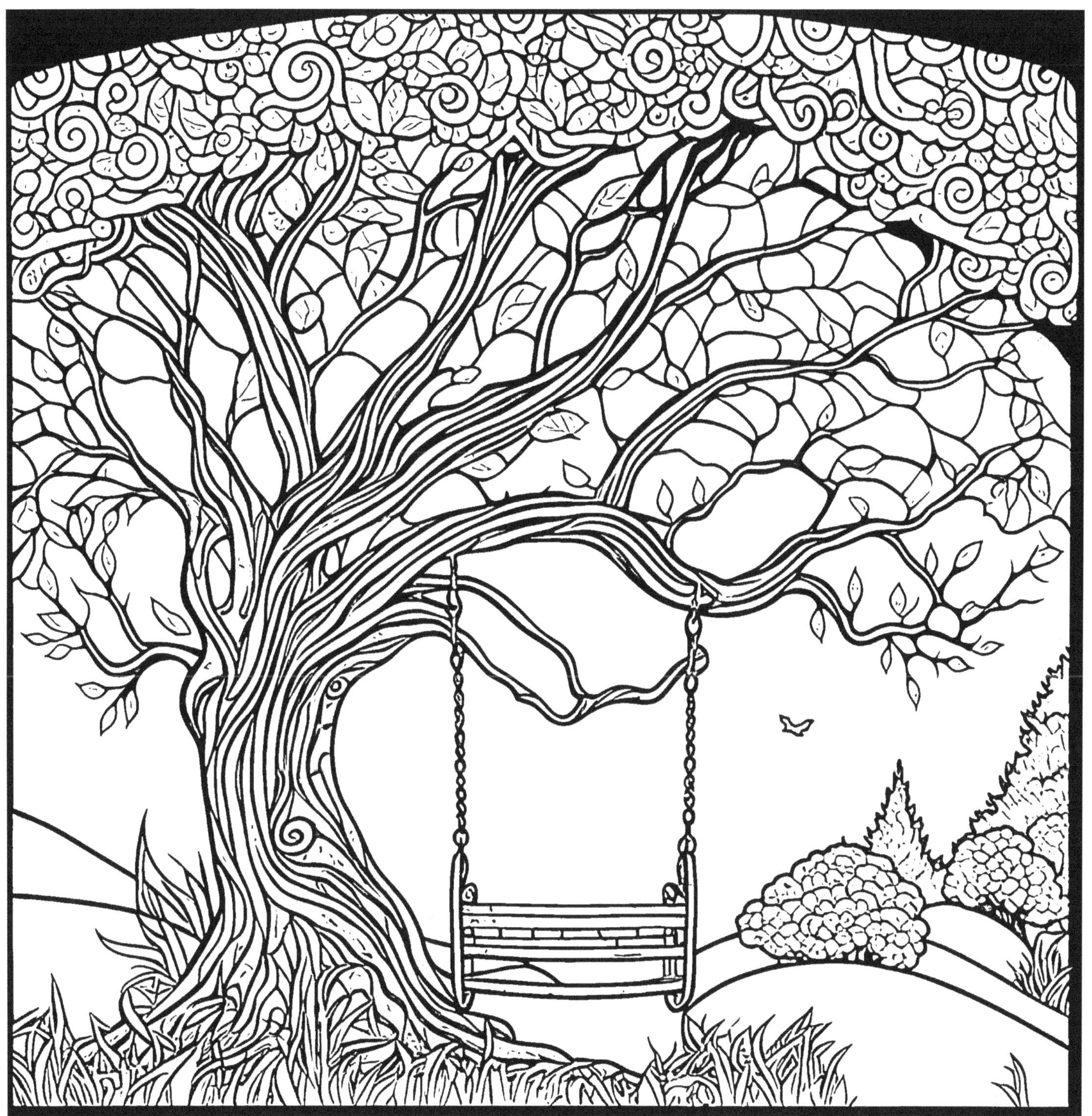

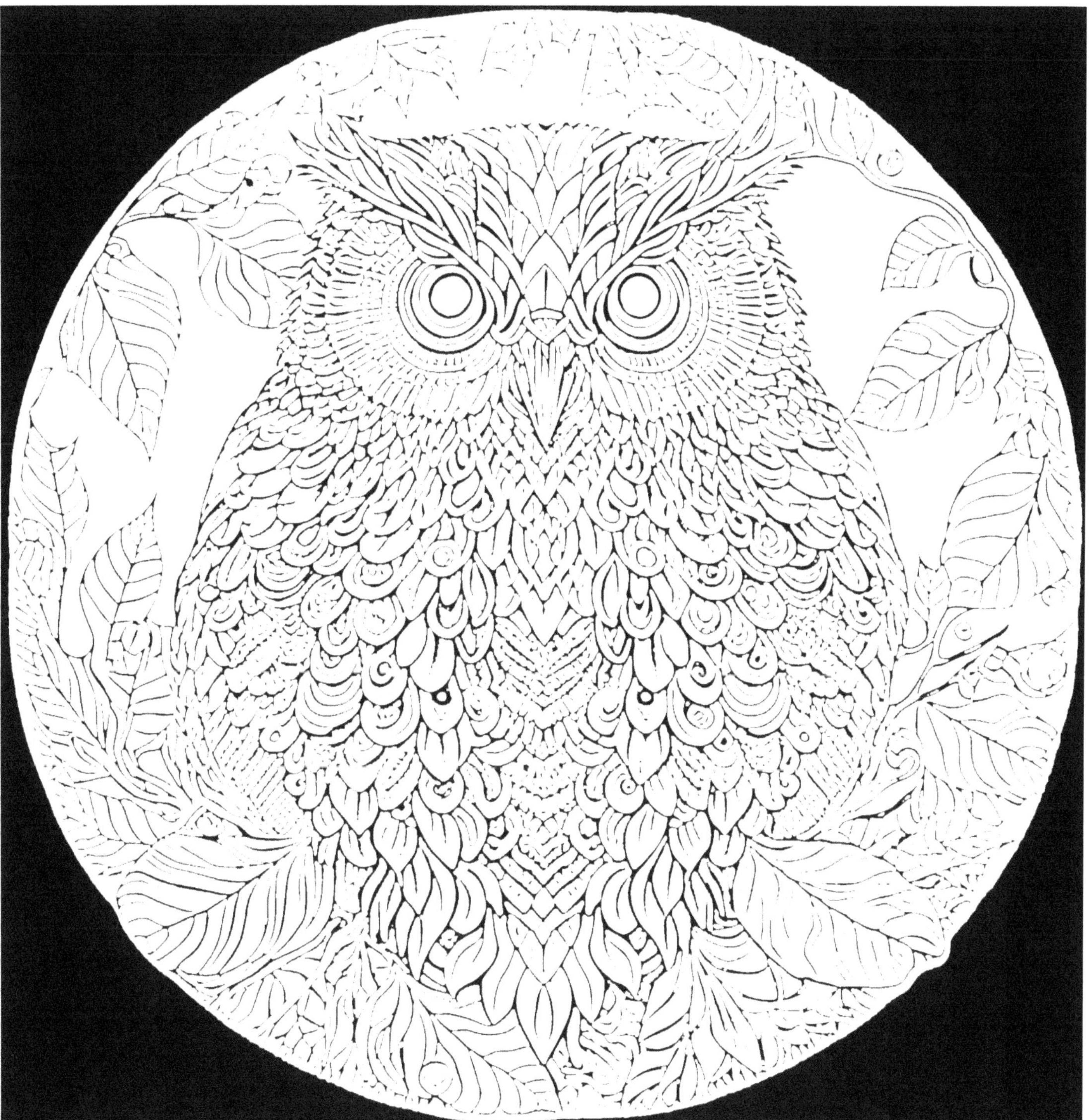

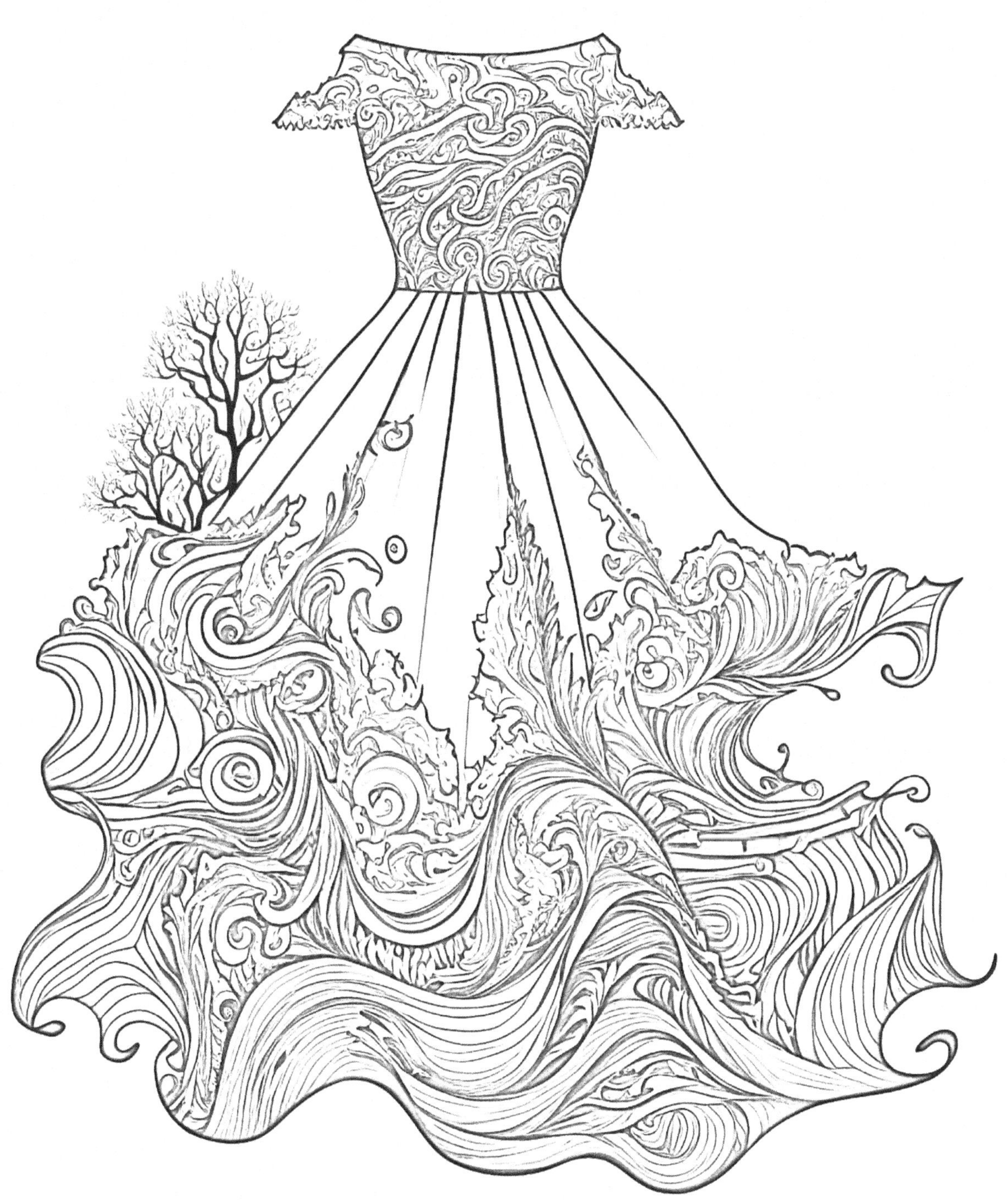

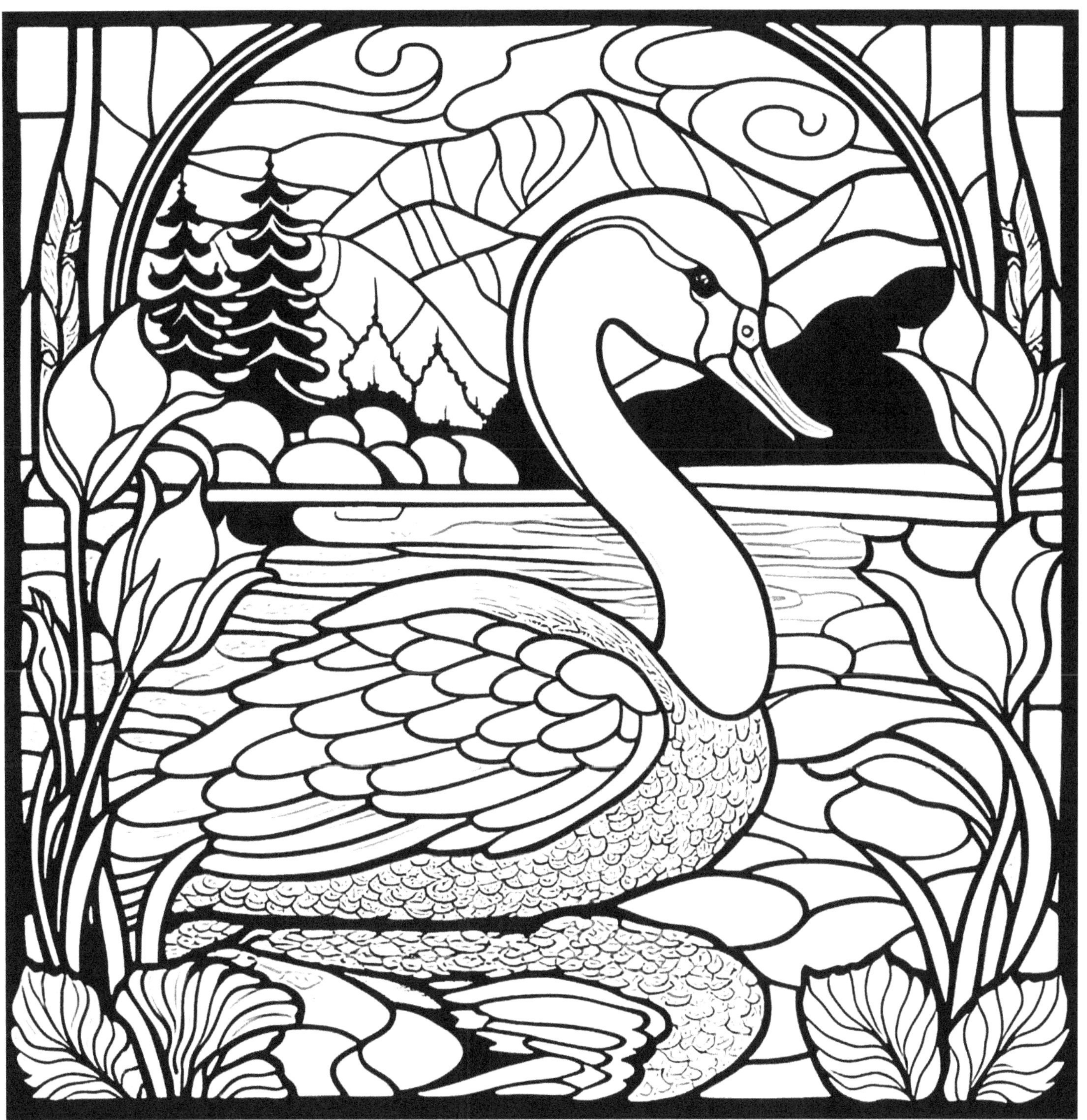

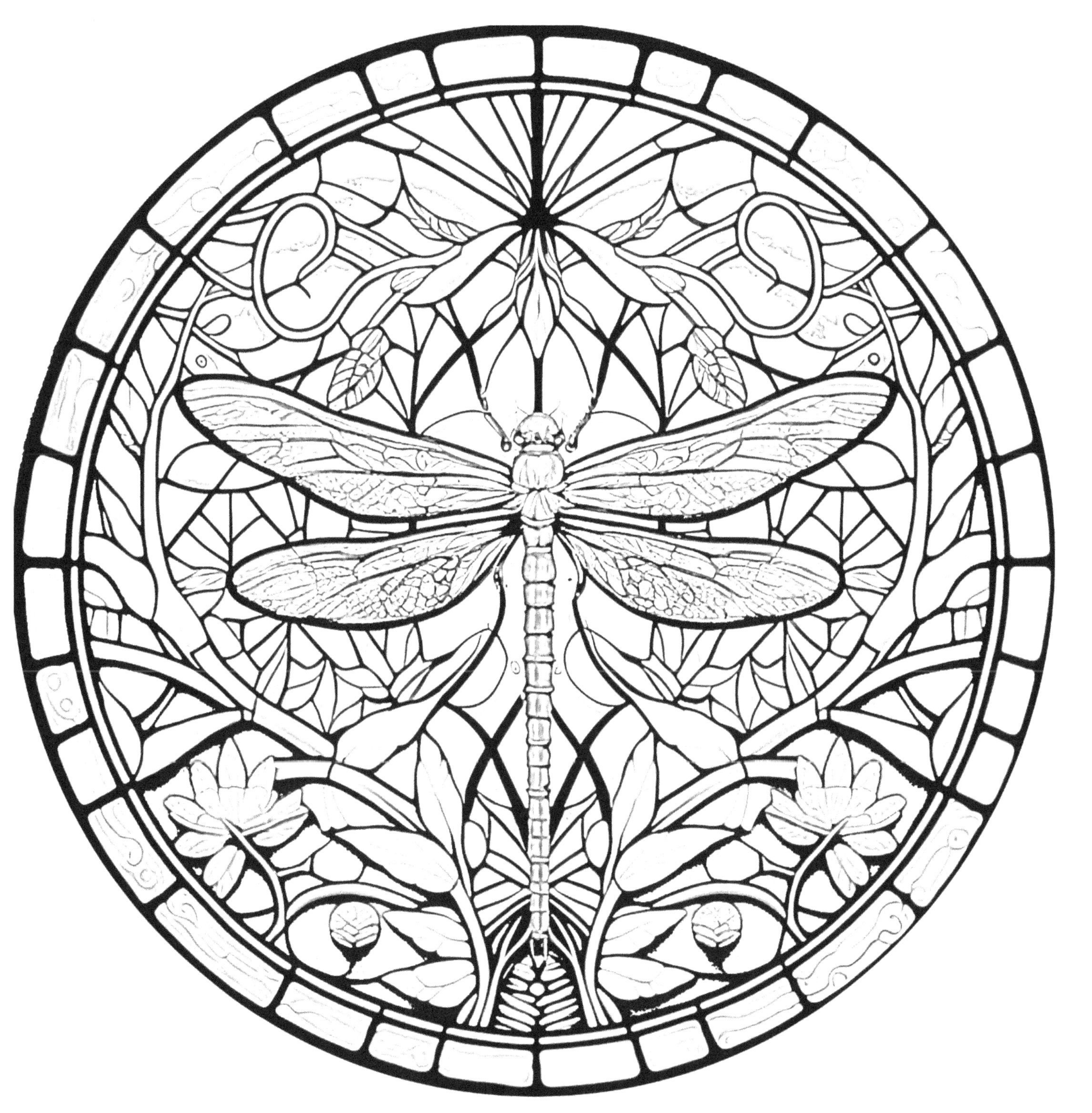

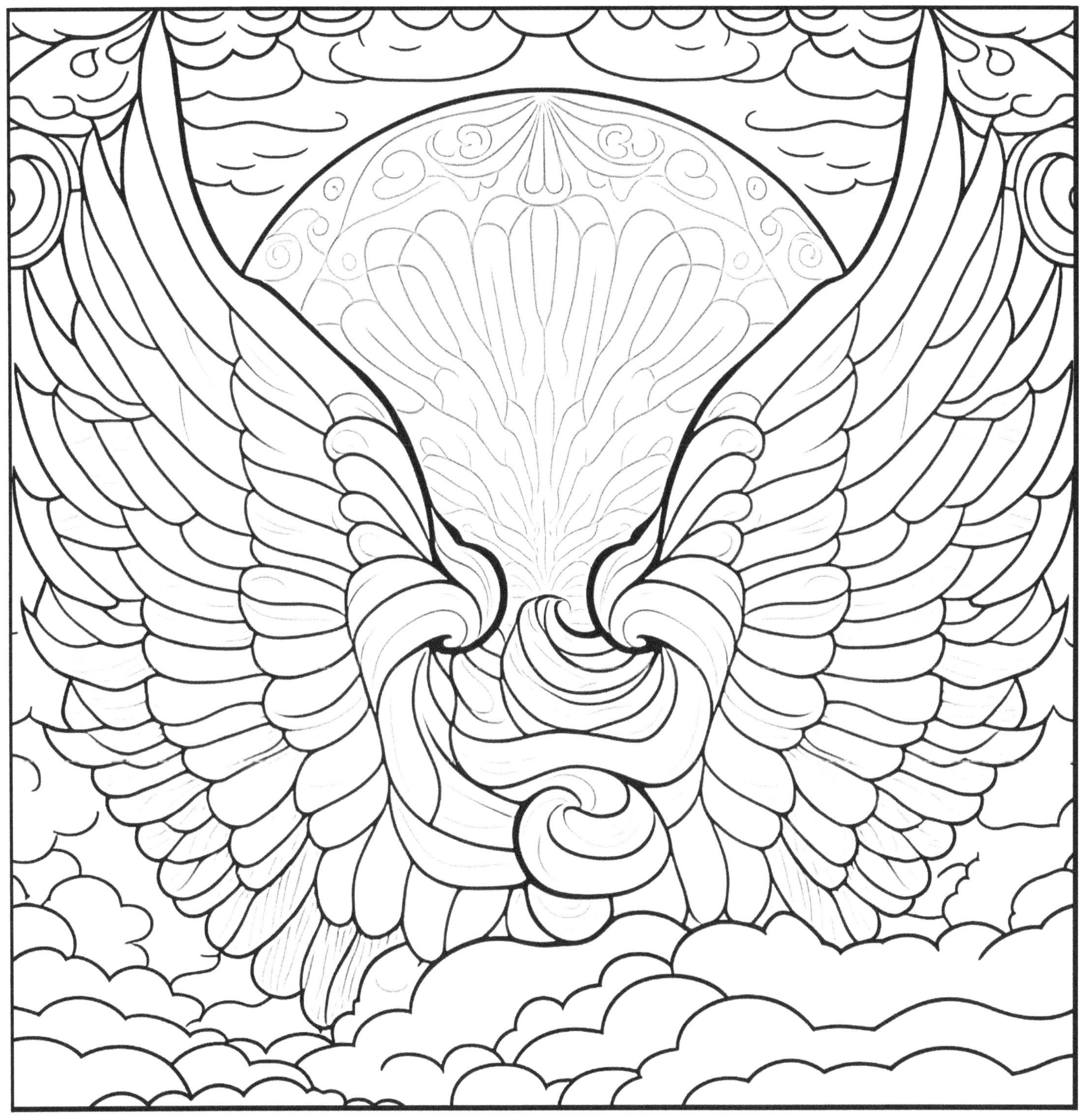

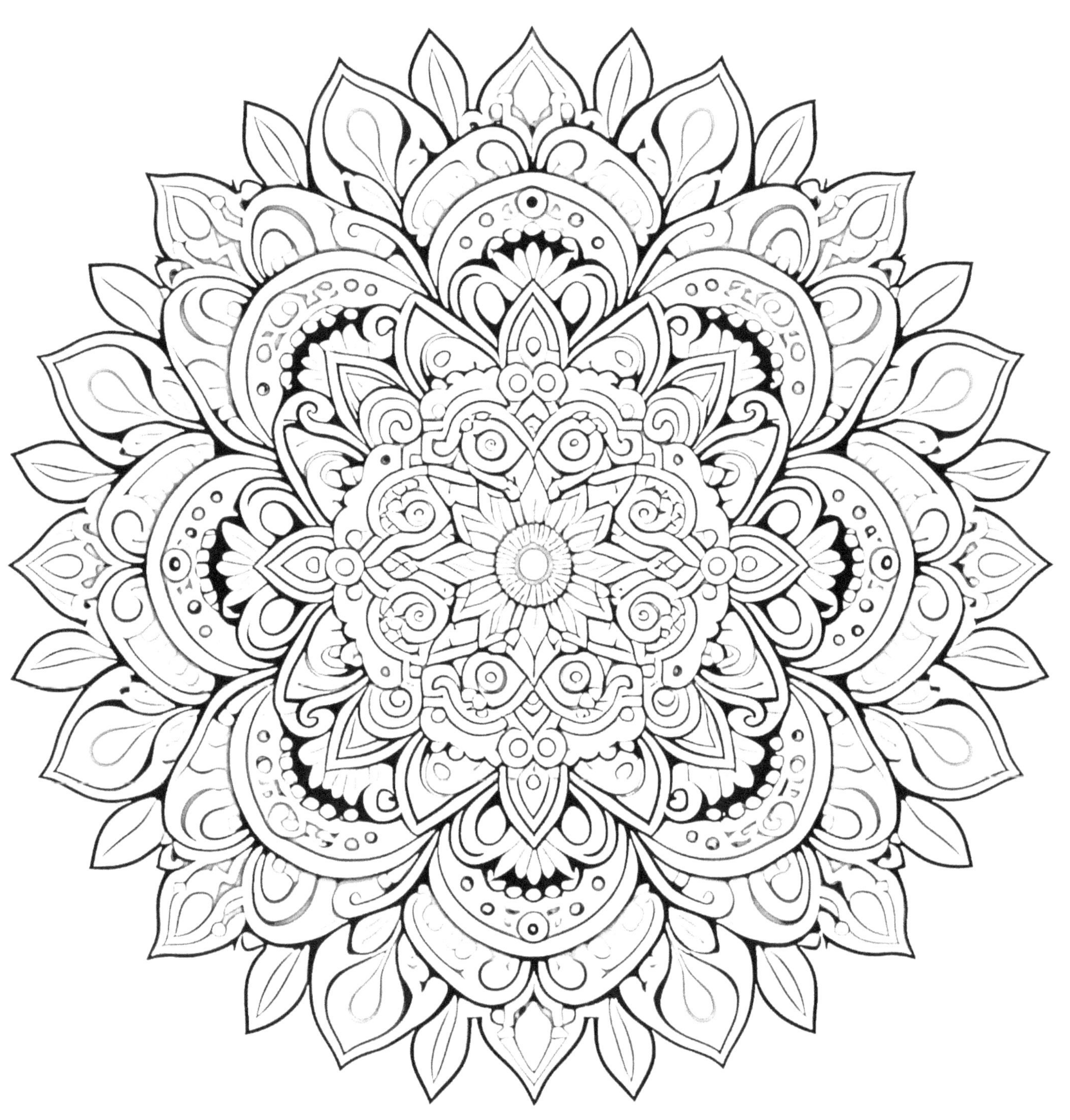

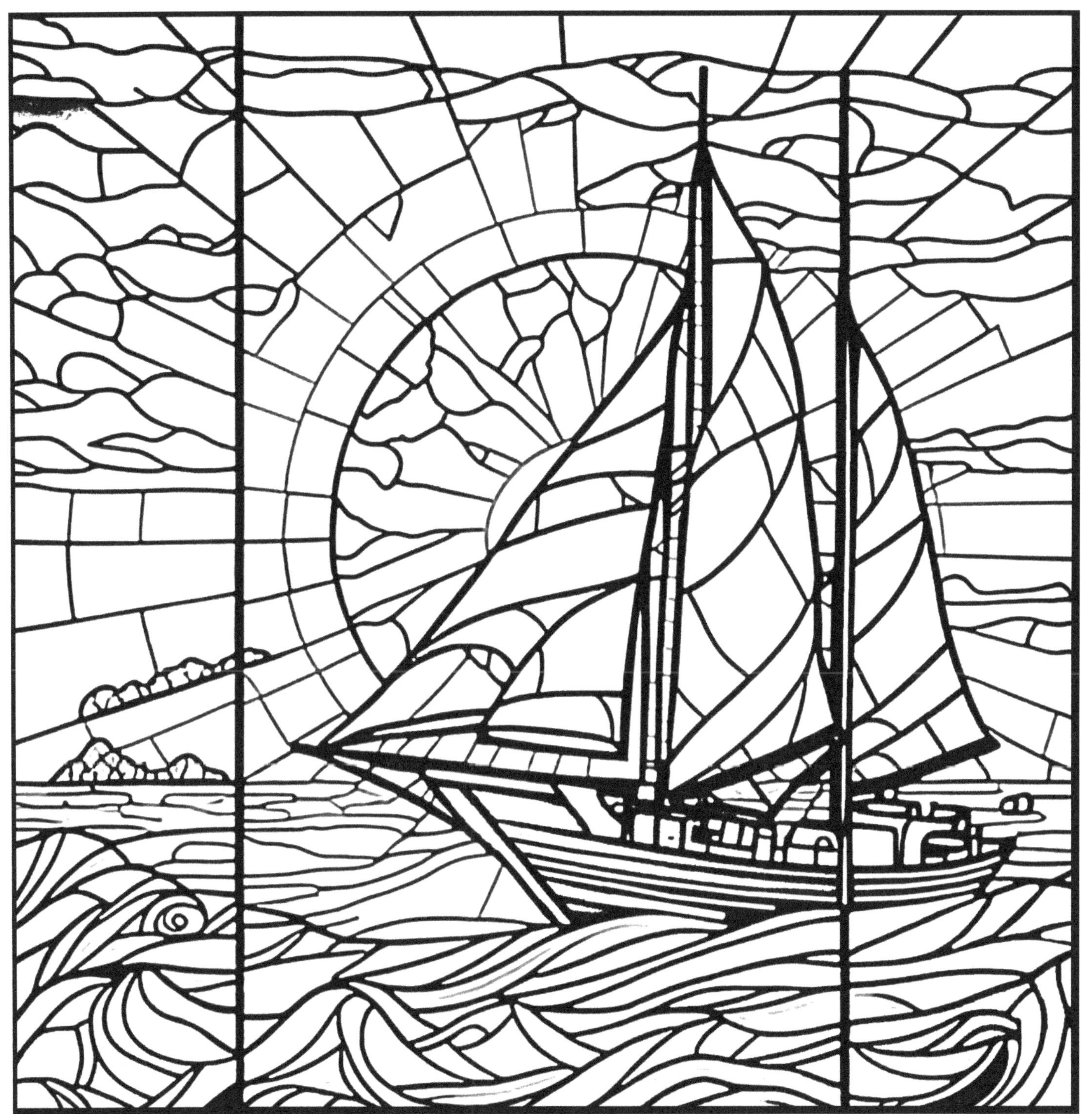

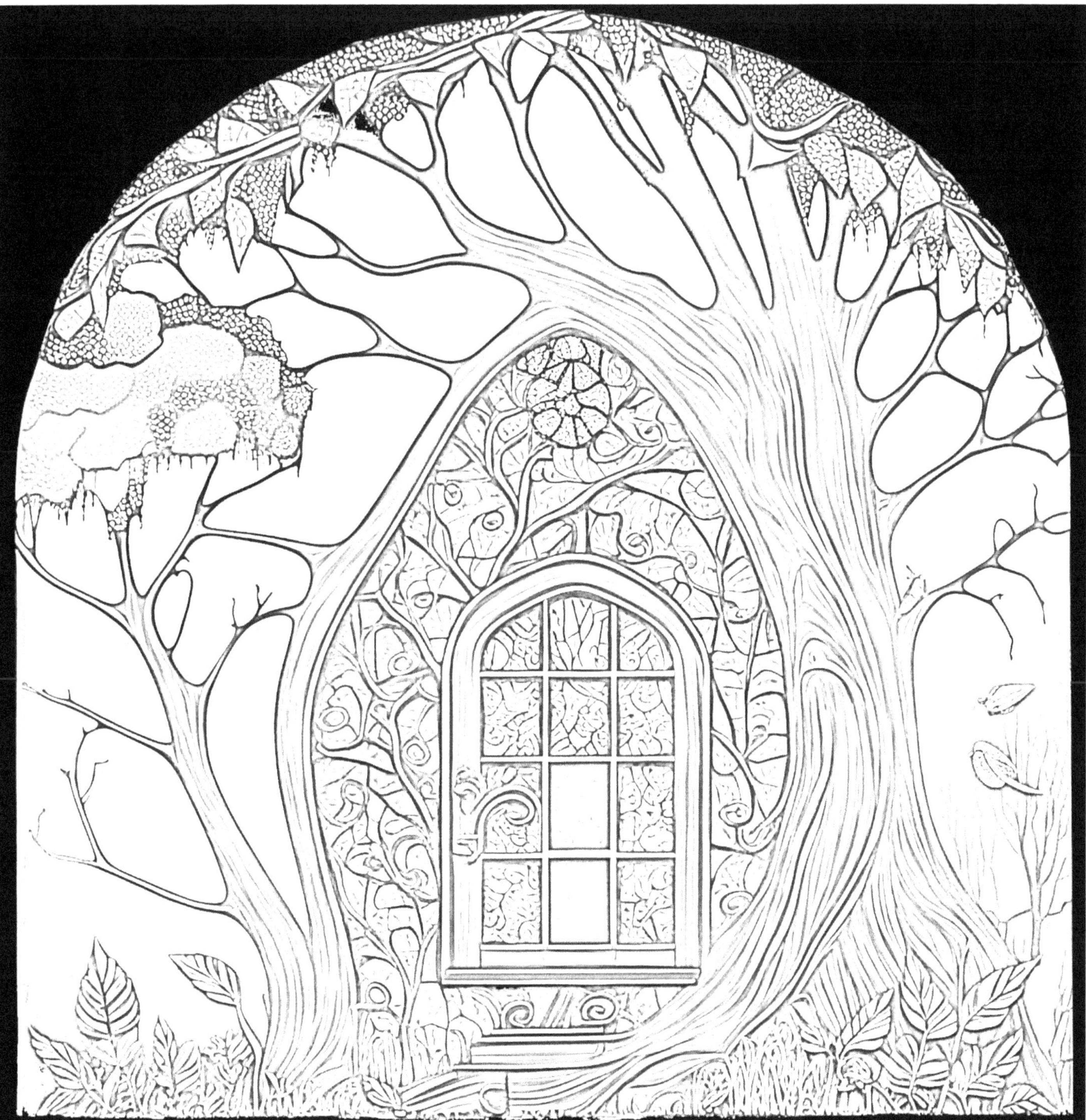

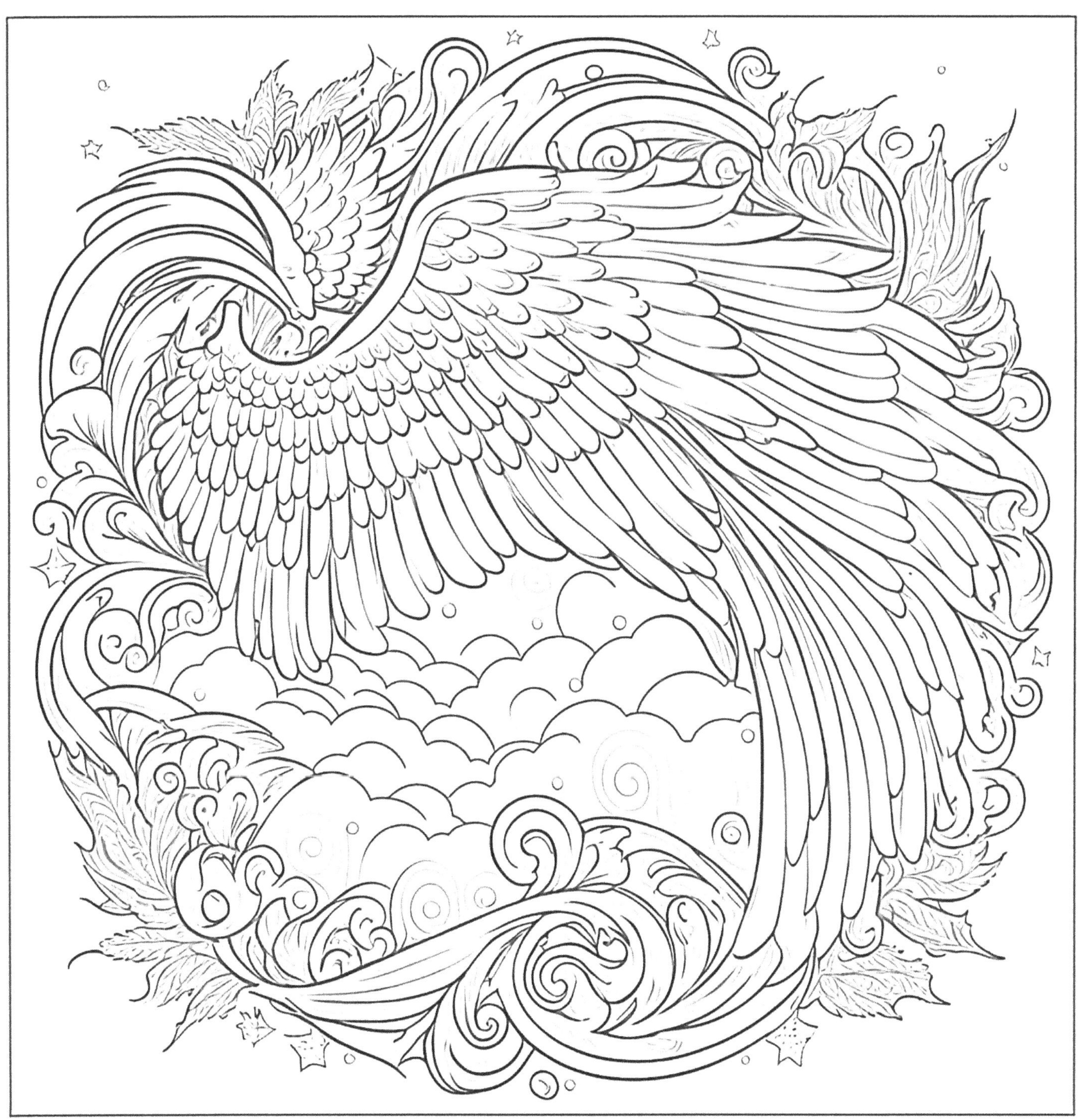

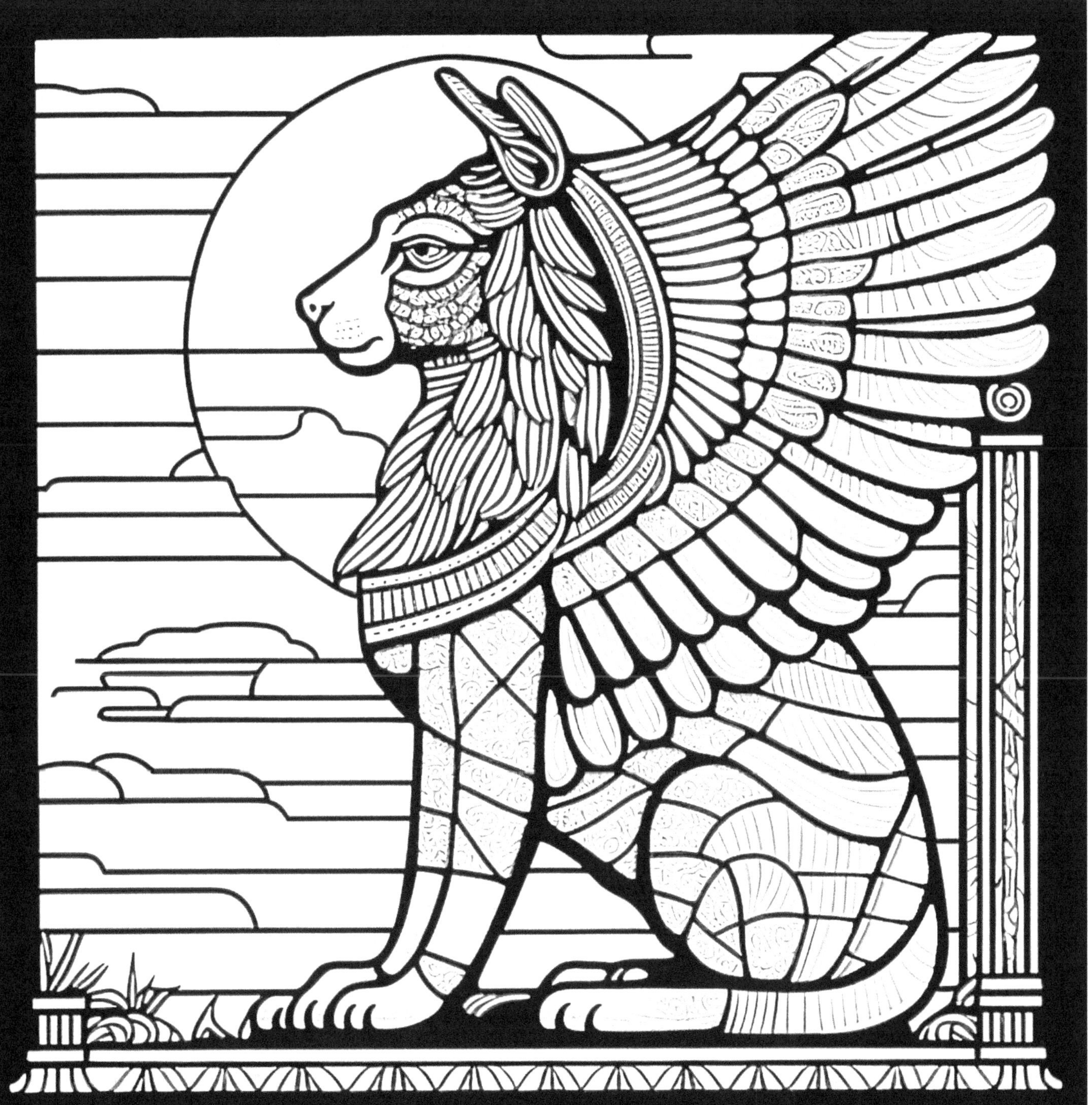

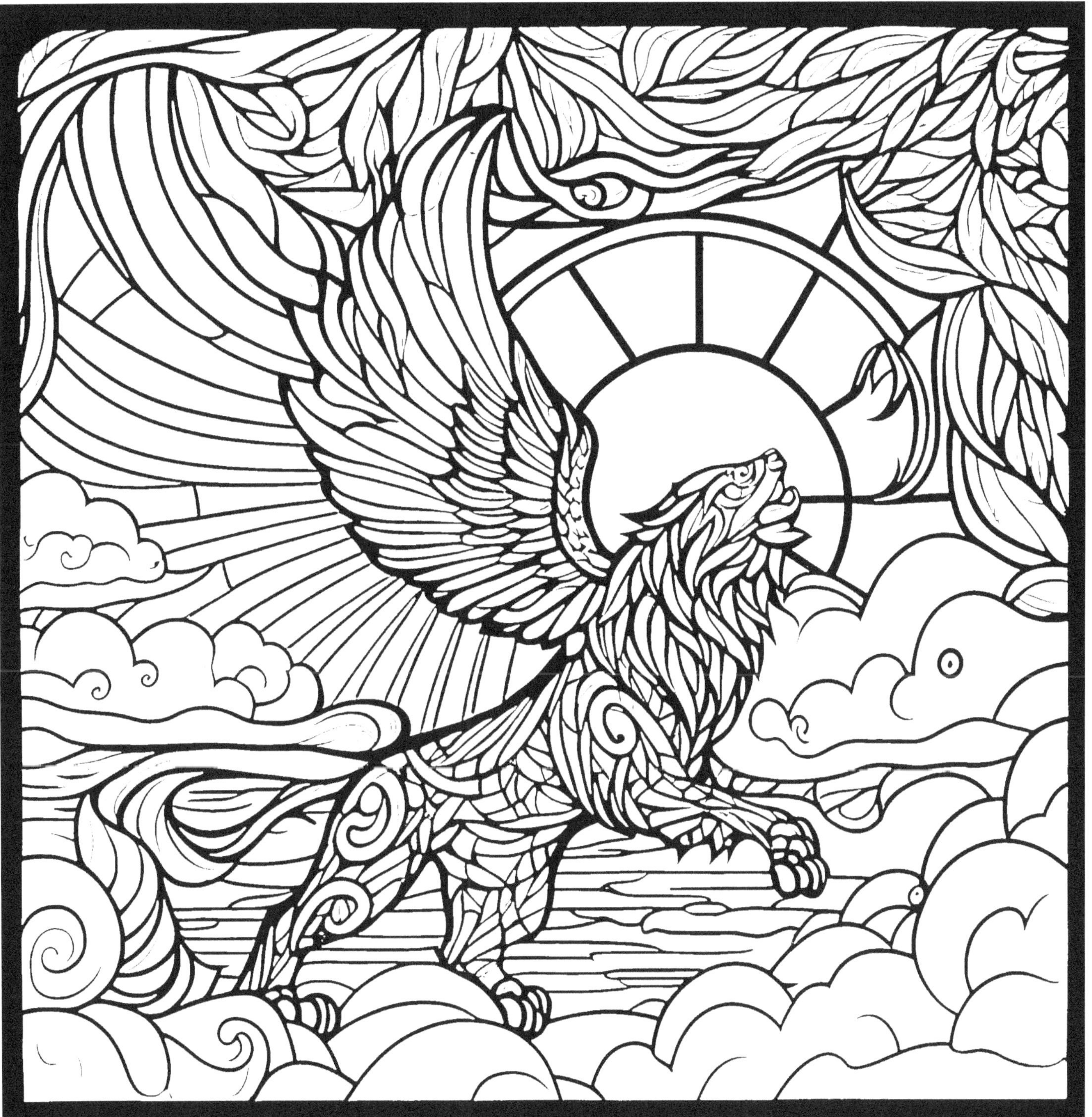

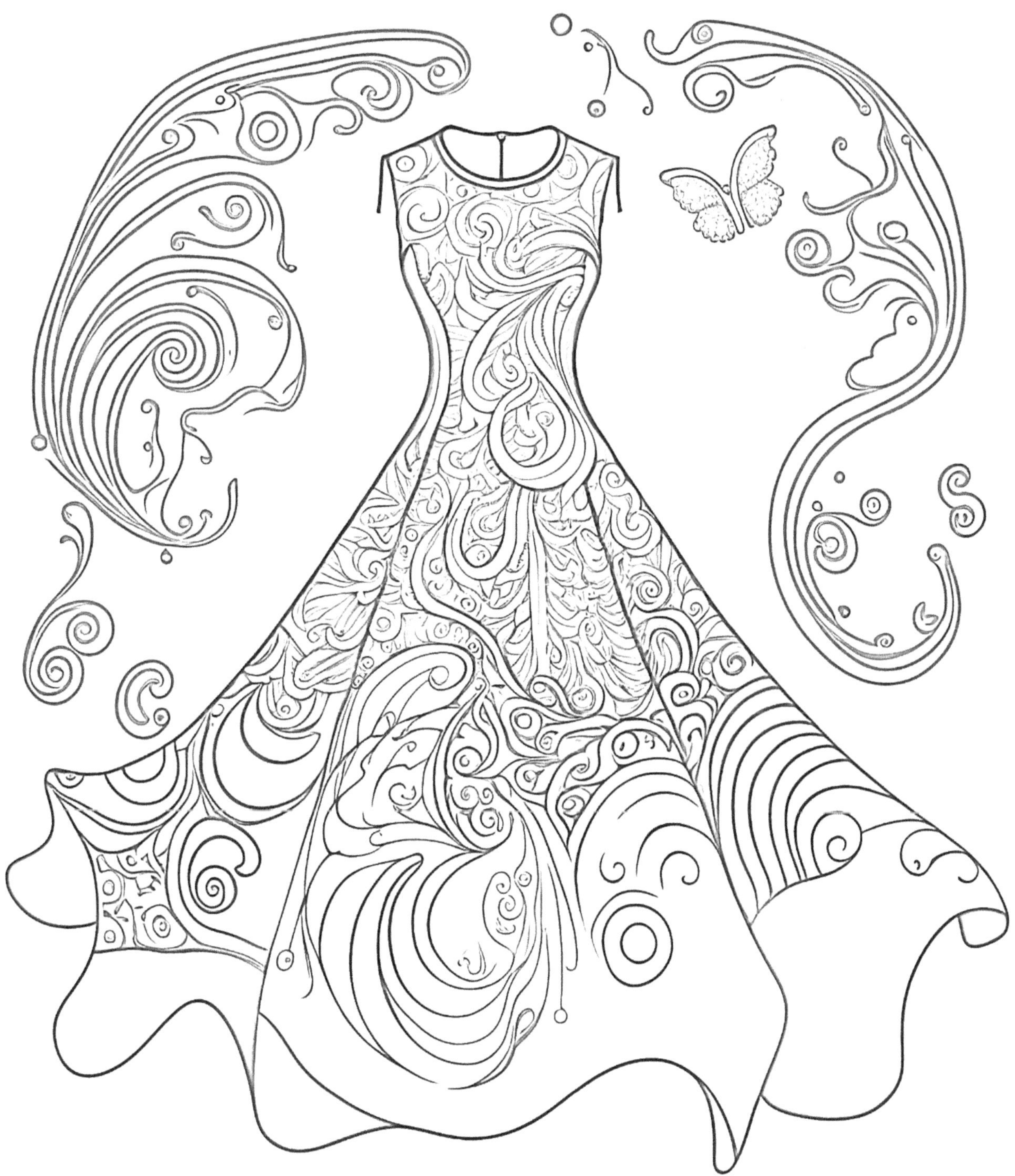

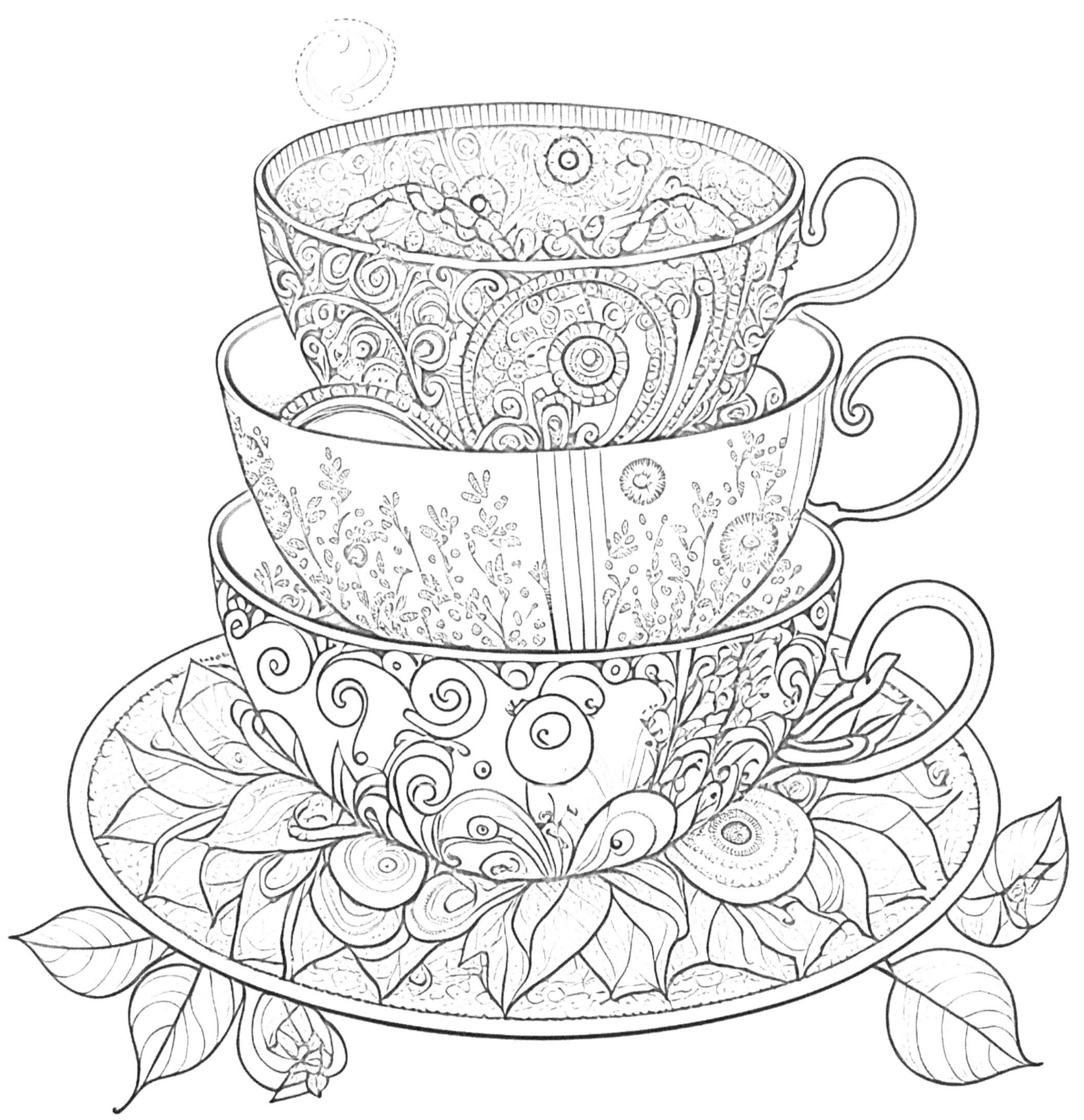

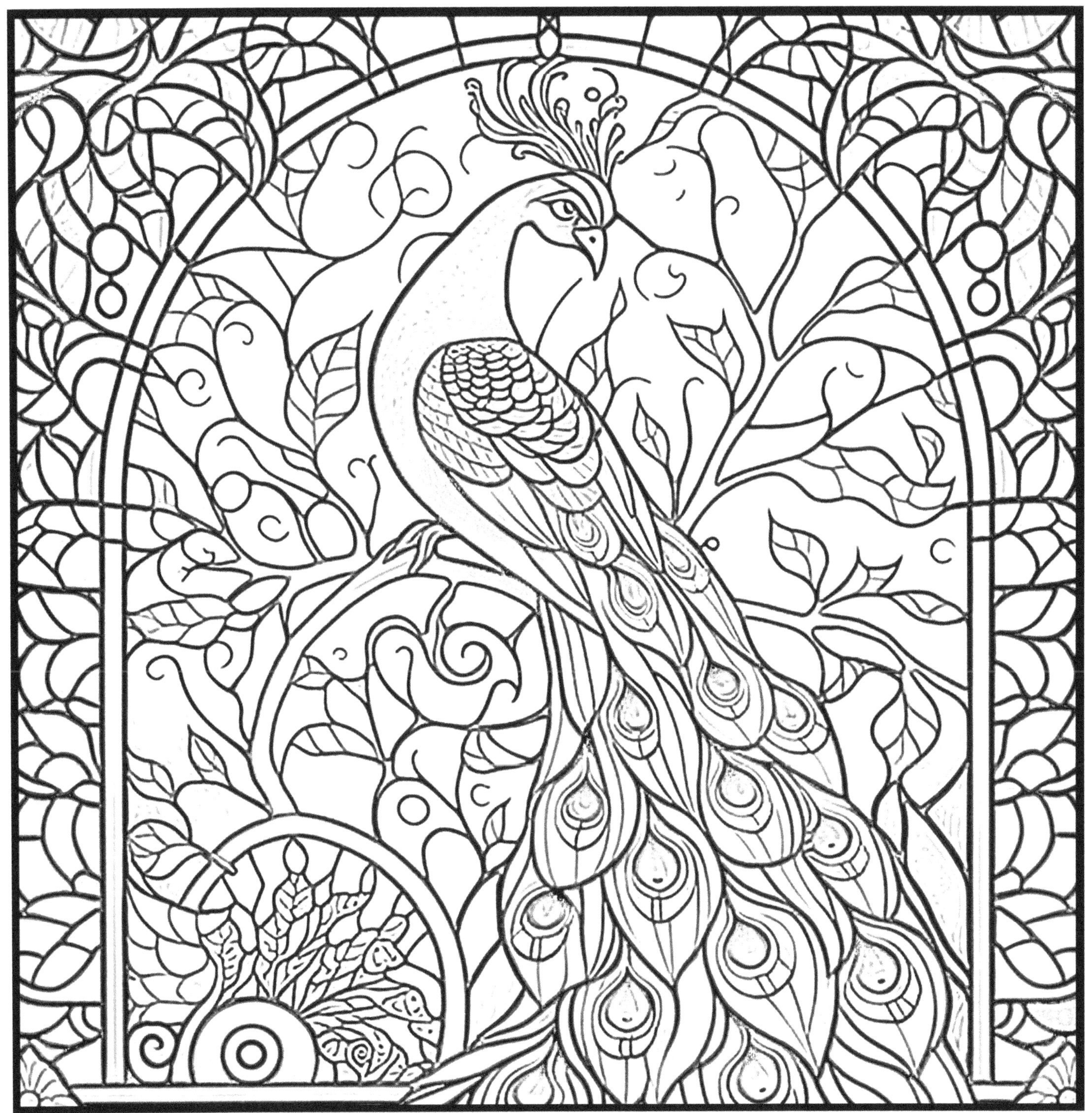

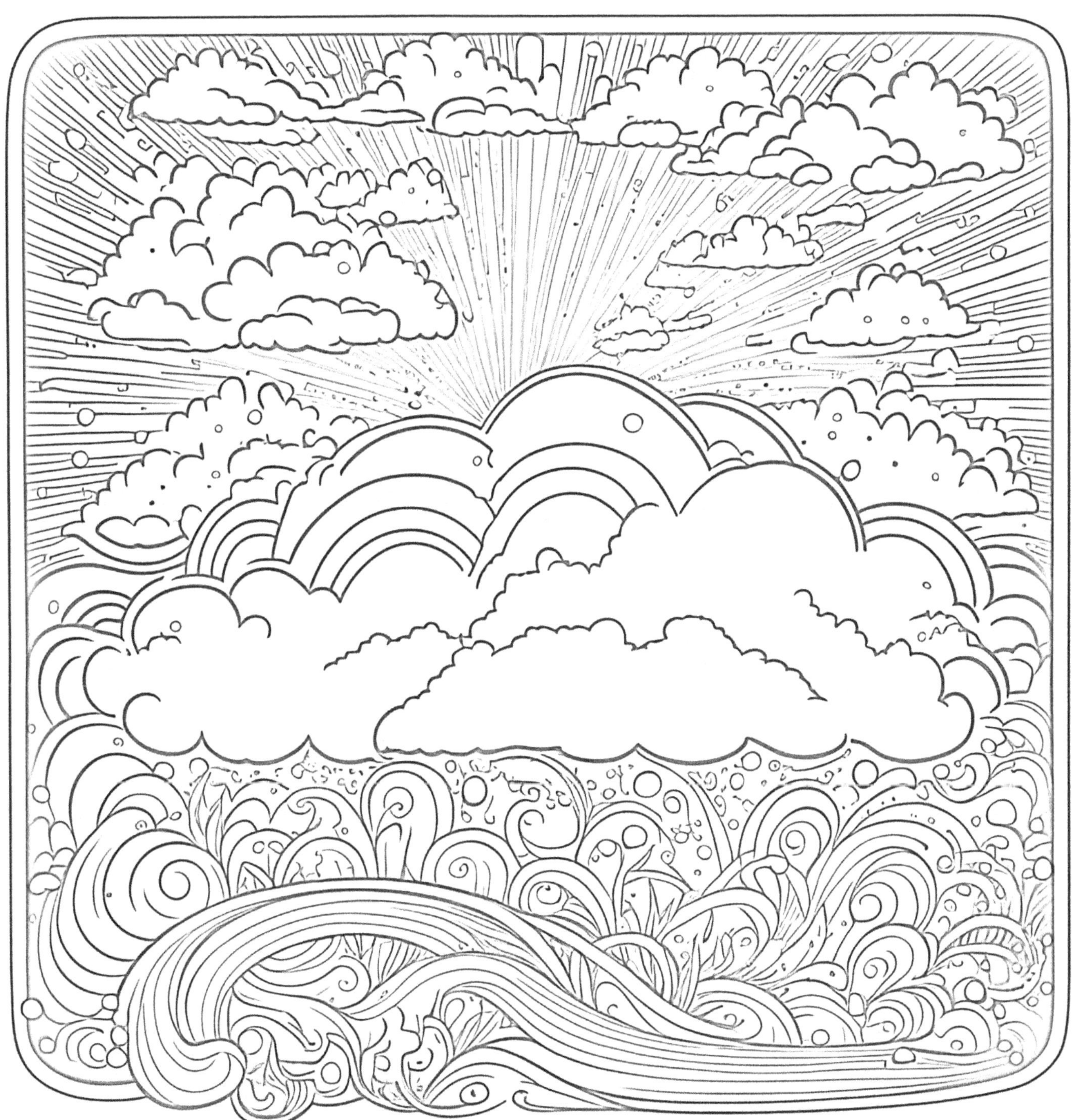

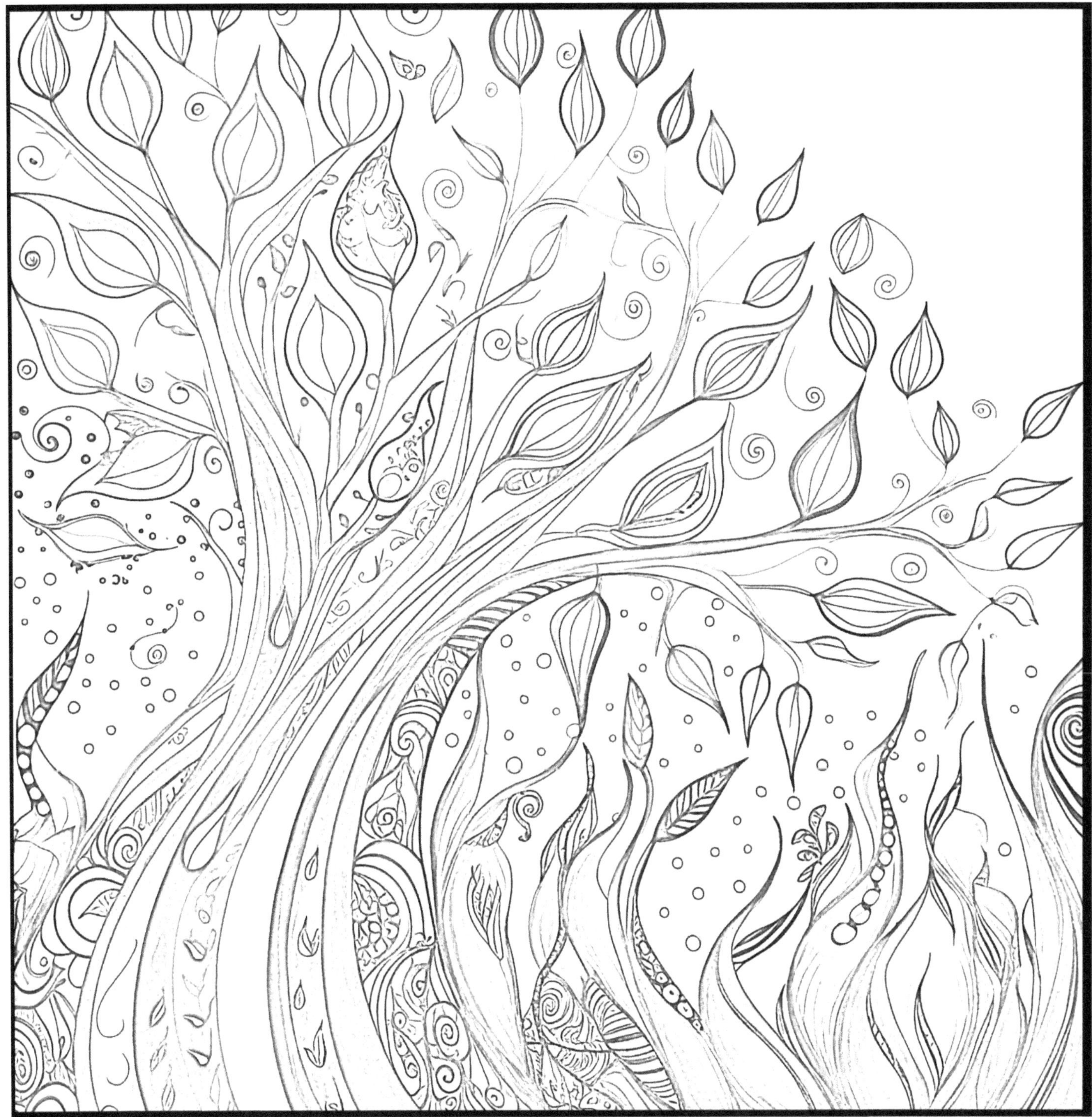

More Coloring Books

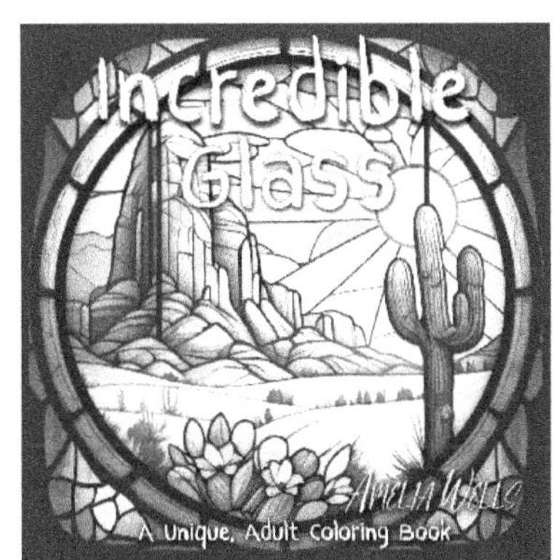

Incredible Glass
9781946501615

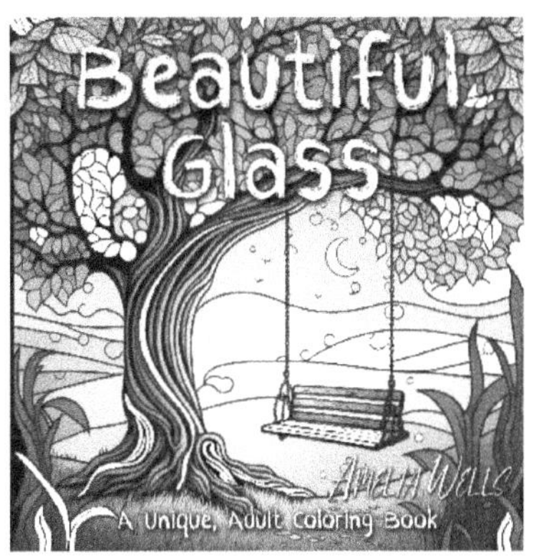

Beautiful Glass
9781946501608

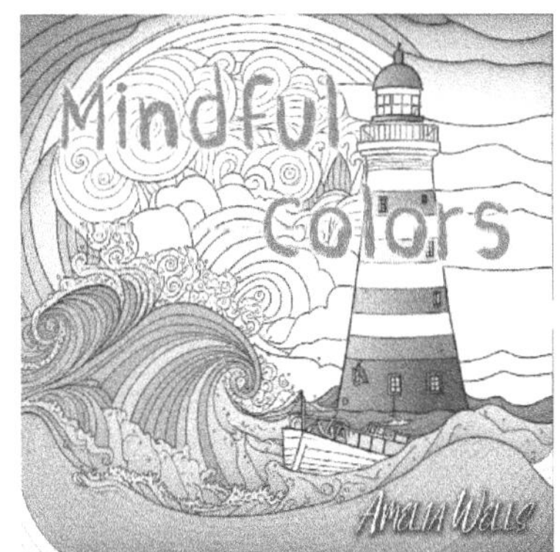

Mindful Colors
9781946501585

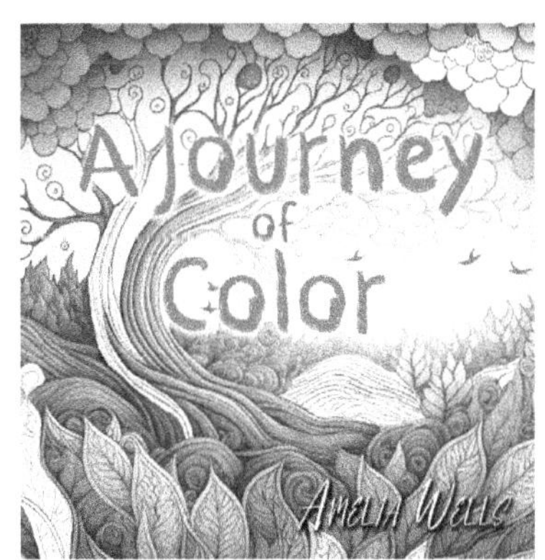

A Journey of Color
9781946501578

About the Illustrator

Amelia is a talented artist and illustrator, known for her intricate and detailed designs. Her passion for art began at a young age and she has been honing her skills ever since. She has a particular love for coloring and has created many coloring books for adults.

Amelia's work is inspired by nature, with a focus on botanical illustrations and patterns. She believes that coloring is a form of meditation and wants to help people relax and unwind through her books.

When she's not creating new coloring pages, Amelia enjoys spending time in nature and traveling. She loves to explore new places and is always on the lookout for inspiration for her next project.

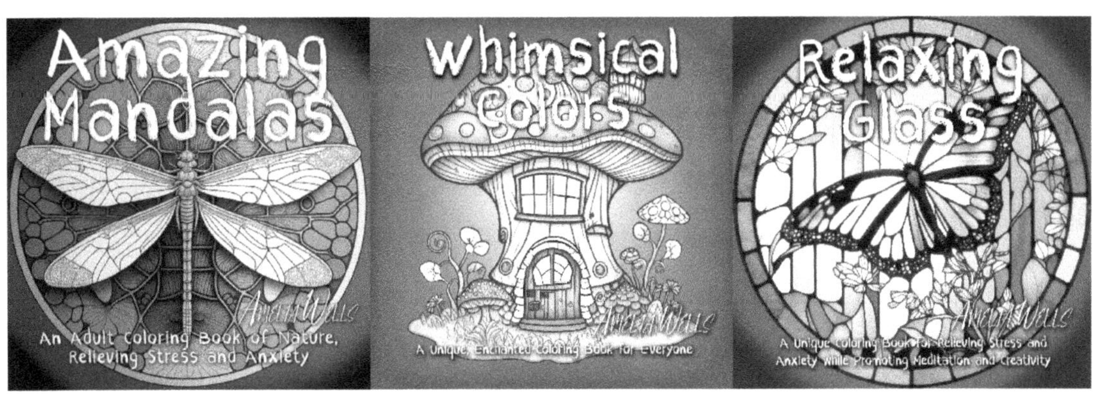

Thank You For the Support

And We Hope You Enjoyed the Book

Share you pictures and feedback: Coloring@tinyfoxpress.com

*Be sure to pop over to www.tinyfoxpress.com to find even more books to color!
Or follow Amelia on Amazon and grab another with the QR code below:*

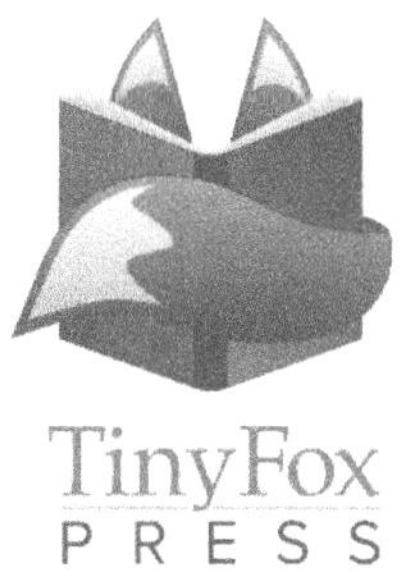

TinyFox
PRESS